To Believe in Freedom

A Mother's Journey From War To Hope

By

Sekip Surget

To Believe in Freedom

Dedication

To the survivors of the Vietnam War, and to the memory of those who did not survive it. This book honors the millions of Vietnamese civilians whose lives were shattered after 1975, when the fall of Saigon marked not just an end, but a beginning, of exile, of uncertainty, of resilience,

To the families who fled by boat, by foot, and by faith, risking all to seek freedom beyond borders, your courage reshaped the course of history.

To the men, women, and children who perished at sea, in camps, or in silence, forever longing for a home left behind, your stories will not be forgotten.

And to May, and to all families like hers, whose quiet strength carried generations forward, this book is a tribute to your unbreakable spirit.

With most profound respect and remembrance,
Sekip Surget

"She carried more than her children, she carried the hope of generations."

, From To Believe in Freedom

Author's Note

To Believe in Freedom is inspired by real events and reflects the experiences of many Vietnamese families who fled their homeland after the fall of Saigon in 1975.

While the characters and dialogue have been fictionalized for narrative clarity and emotional depth, the events described, the boat escapes, the refugee camps in Malaysia, and the difficult adjustment to life in America, are based on documented histories and survivor testimonies.

Some names, locations, and timelines have been altered or combined for the sake of storytelling. Any resemblance to actual individuals is purely coincidental unless explicitly acknowledged.

I wrote this story to honor the strength of the Vietnamese diaspora and to shed light on a chapter of history that still echoes in the hearts of many.

Table of Contents

Chapter 1

The War That Changed Everything

The Vietnam War didn't begin with a sudden declaration or the arrival of marching armies. It started quietly, a buildup of ideas that simmered over generations. These were ideas of freedom from foreign rule, of self-determination, and of shaping a future in the shadow of global powers. For nearly a century, Vietnam bore the weight of colonial control: first under the French, who exploited its land for rubber and rice, and later under the looming pressure of the Cold War.

By the 1950s, the world had split in two. On one side stood the democratic West, led by the United States, with promises of liberty and capitalism. On the other hand, the communist bloc was dominated by the Soviet Union and a rising China. Vietnam, a narrow, river-laced country of rice paddies and thick jungles, sat at the heart of this ideological clash. The nation itself was split not just on a map, but in spirit. The North, hardened by resistance and rooted in its cause, embraced communism. The South, unstable and politically fragile, leaned toward the West in search of a different future.

The division became official in 1954 after the Viet Minh, communist forces led by Ho Chi Minh, defeated the French at Dien Bien Phu, a brutal siege that shocked the world. France gave up its colonial ambitions, and the Geneva Accords split the country along the 17th parallel. The North, centered in Hanoi, moved forward with communist support from Moscow and Beijing. The South, based in Saigon under President Ngo Dinh Diem, was backed by the United States. But Diem's regime was weak from the start, plagued by corruption, nepotism, and harsh repression.

What began as a war for independence turned into a proxy conflict, fueled by Cold War fears. The U.S., convinced of the "domino theory" the belief that if South Vietnam fell, the rest of Southeast Asia would follow began investing heavily. Under President John F. Kennedy, the U.S. increased aid and sent military advisors to train South Vietnamese troops. The hope was to win the war without sending in American combat forces. But war has its own momentum. After Kennedy's assassination in 1963,

President Lyndon B. Johnson inherited the crisis. His vision for a "Great Society" at home was soon eclipsed by war abroad.

In August 1964, the Gulf of Tonkin incident changed everything. Reports that North Vietnamese boats had attacked U.S. destroyers gave Johnson the justification he needed. Whether the event was misinterpreted or manipulated, it led to congressional approval for expanded military action. Johnson, convinced that U.S. credibility was at stake, ordered troops into Vietnam. In March 1965, 3,500 Marines landed at Da Nang. It was the beginning of full-scale war. By the late 1960s, over 500,000 American troops were in-country

For those on the ground, the war wasn't theory; it was life. For millions of Vietnamese civilians, it meant running from bombings, hiding from ambushes, and living in fear. Villages were burned. Fields were cratered. Families scattered. Schools became shelters. Markets disappeared. The familiar turned to ruin.

Among the many families affected was that of May, a mother who once lived by the quiet rhythms of rural life. Her days were filled with the smell of rice steaming, the feel of wet soil, the laughter of her children, and her husband's stories at night. But then the war took him. Like many

Southern men, he was drafted and never returned. Left alone in a land where danger could come from any direction, May had to make impossible choices.

But she wouldn't give in. As the airstrikes came closer and fear swallowed her village, she decided to act. With only her love to guide her, May carried her children across rivers, through war zones, and past enemy lines. What she did wasn't driven by politics or ideology; a mother determined to keep her family alive. This is her story.

Chapter 2

The Last Days Before the Fall

It was the last week of April 1975, just days before the world would awaken to the fall of Saigon. In the small Mekong Delta town of Vĩnh Long, seventy kilometers downriver from the capital, life clung to a thin illusion of normalcy. A fragile calm stretched over a deep chasm of fear. Beneath this veneer, tension gripped every muddy street, every tin-roofed home, every soul tightening like a vice with each passing day.

The evening air hung thick and humid, carrying a cruel contrast of scents. The sweetness of Easter lilies and coffee blossoms, symbols of peace and renewal, mingled with the earthy smells of charcoal fires and wet delta soil. A sluggish breeze stirred the banana trees, making tattered laundry flutter like surrender flags. As the sun sank, the sky ignited in streaks of orange and bruised purple, casting long, shifting shadows over the dirt roads.

Children, barefoot and dusty, kicked a half-deflated rubber ball through the alleyways, their laughter rising in bright bursts against the weight of dusk. Their joy clashed with the distant pop-pop-pop of gunfire beyond the rice paddies, and the low, chest-rattling thunder of artillery rolling over the flatlands. These sounds never stopped; they were the war's background hum, a second, sinister heartbeat beneath daily life.

In front of a wooden house with a rust-streaked metal roof, a group of neighbors huddled on low stools around a battered radio. The old device sputtered and hissed with static, its voice trying to bridge a crumbling nation. At last, a clipped, official voice cut through: "South Vietnamese forces are holding firm against communist aggression in the defense of Saigon. Reinforcements are being marshaled. Citizens are urged to remain calm and stay in their homes."

No one believed it. They had lived through too much to be fooled now. The circle exchanged quiet, knowing glances. A woman clutched a rosary, her fingers rubbing the beads in a rapid, mechanical rhythm. A man exhaled a long plume of smoke; his eyes fixed on the burning tip of his cigarette. They didn't need radio lies. They had seen the truth in the hollow faces of retreating ARVN soldiers: Saigon was surrounded. Saigon was collapsing.

The final Iron Gate of Xuân Lộc had fallen on April 20. Everyone knew it was the last line. There was nothing left to stop the North.

The elders sat silent, their faces carved with the weight of past wars: against the French, the Japanese, and now this. Some had once worn French colonial uniforms. Others had briefly believed in American promises of air support, reconstruction, and freedom. Now those promises were ashes. Rumors swirled: rooftop helicopter evacuations, ghost ships slipping out of harbors at night, the last flights packed with desperate families and vanishing hope.

Inside a nearby home, May held her youngest son, Trong, cradling him in her gentle arms, which trembled from exhaustion. His body was warm against her chest; his little arms curled around her neck. His eyes were heavy with sleep, too young to know fear, but close enough to feel the frantic rhythm of her heart.

On the wooden floor nearby sat Hoang, her fifteen-year-old. He was caught in that awful space between child and man. His legs were crossed; his gaze locked on the radio as if searching the static for a hidden truth. His face was too serious, too knowing for his age. He understood what was coming, but part of him still hoped it might not.

May's eyes drifted to the corner of the room, where all their possessions were reduced to a few pitiful bundles: two sacks of rice, a jar of dried shrimp, a near-empty bottle of aspirin, and an envelope with a few crumpled bills. Her chest clenched. How long could she stretch what little they had? How could she feed nine children alone?

Her husband had been taken months ago during a raid near Nha Trang, accused of sympathizing with the wrong side. They said he was in Trại Nam Hà, a re-education camp deep in the jungle, known for disease, starvation, and silence. She hadn't heard a word since. Not when their last child, baby Ngoc, was born in November. She had whispered her name into the damp night air. No answer had come.

Now, in the dim kitchen, May counted a few coins in her palm. Cold. Useless. The food cupboard was nearly bare: the last grains of rice, a handful of anchovies, oil dregs. She had nothing left to trade. Each market trip brought fresh humiliation, soaring prices, and pitying looks from the vendors.

Outside, the children's voices rang out, a bright defiance against the twilight. They didn't know yet. Not fully. Not like she did.

Inside, May blinked back tears and stirred their dinner, nine bowls of plain rice with a few garden

8

vegetables. She laid them on the table with deliberate care, each motion a quiet prayer. She had heard the escape rumors, boats leaving by night, smugglers asking for gold. But she had no gold, only her children. The roads were clogged with families like hers, fleeing with their pots, mats, and infants, hoping for a miracle.

The war had reached them. It was in the quiet pantry, in the empty mailbox, in the way the children no longer asked about their father.

That night, as they came in from play, dusty, smiling, loud, May forced a smile too. It was tired, but it was real. This, at least, she could still give. She handed out bowls, kissed foreheads, whispered comforts she didn't believe. Everything outside was crumbling.

But inside her home, she served dinner anyway. It was her last defense: an act of love, of defiance, and impossible hope in the face of everything.

Chapter 3

The Volkswagen Beetle

Just as the family settled around the low wooden table, bowls of rice still steaming, a sound shattered the fragile stillness. An engine sputtered in the distance, struggling, choking, growing louder as it crawled in from the dark. No headlights pierced the heavy night, only the slow crunch of tires on dry gravel. It sounded like grinding teeth, like fate creeping forward one inch at a time.

Out of the shadows, a battered, olive-drab Volkswagen Beetle lurched into the faint glow of a streetlamp. Its frame rattled as though it might fall apart, then screeched to a halt, the engine coughing in a final spasm before idling in nervous fits. The driver's door flew open with a metallic wail, and a figure burst out, moving too fast.

"Má!" The voice cut sharply through the air. "Má, where are you?" Minh. Her eldest son.

His tall silhouette emerged uniform, creased, and soaked with sweat, mud clinging to his boots. He didn't walk, he charged. When he reached the door, he was a storm: breathless, frantic, his soldier's hands rough as he gripped his mother's arm, the urgency radiating off him. *"We have to go,"* he said flatly. *"Now."* May's stomach dropped. The moment she'd feared had arrived. For weeks, she had felt it drawing near, but now, it felt like being shoved off a ledge into a world that no longer made sense.

She looked past him at the tiny, trembling Beetle. "What happened?" she asked, already knowing. "Saigon is gone," Minh said. "It's over. The North is pushing south. Vĩnh Long is next, maybe a day, maybe hours. If we don't leave now, we won't be able to get out at all."

Her breath caught. She glanced at the pantry. Her hands clenched instinctively. She thought of the sacks of rice, the hidden jewelry beneath the floorboards. The savings. The whispered dreams. All of it is useless now.

She moved automatically, rolling blankets, tying them off with shaking hands, and stacking them near the door. Sang and Trong, just two and four, whined in confusion, rubbing their eyes, clinging to her legs. Time had become razor-thin, every second buzzing with urgency. Minh noticed. He grabbed her arm again, spinning her around. His voice cracked. "Má, we don't have time for this! Forget it! Get in the car!"

May's fear sparked briefly into resistance. "I know," she said, voice firming. "But the children must eat. Just get the car ready. Help me get them inside." She glanced at the tiny car and shook her head. "Ten of us in that? Minh why not something bigger? A truck? Why didn't you steal a helicopter?"

Minh didn't answer. There was no answer. Without a word, he yanked open the passenger door, shoved the front seat forward, then ripped the back seat out entirely, hurling it into the dirt. The Beetle was now a bare, ugly, desperate metal shell. May froze as her children emerged, eyes wide in the dim light. Too many. Far too many. But Minh wasn't thinking about comfort. He was thinking about survival.

"Get in!" he shouted, shoving the first child inside. Chi and Hoang went first, pressing themselves against the cold metal. Then the younger ones passed in like parcels, squeezed into laps, knees against backs. Little Trong sat on Minh's lap behind the wheel. Sang was wedged behind May. Baby Ngoc slept in her arms. They were packed tight, breath and limbs pressed together.

They were ready. Then, from the shadows, a voice called out. "May!" Everyone froze. Mrs. Tran, her best friend, emerged from the darkness, breathless and clutching her six-year-old son Duy's hand. His wide eyes reflected

12

terror. "Take Duy with you," she said. A pause. A collective breath. "Chị, no you have to come! Aren't you leaving?" Mrs. Tran shook her head. "My husband is still in the camp. If I leave, I'll be marked. I may never see him again. But, Duy, he's our only son. He must live." Duy clung to her. "Mẹ, con không muốn đi một mình..." ("I don't want to go alone...") She knelt, hands on his cheeks. "You are our only hope," she whispered. "You must survive. One day, you'll bring us together again." Duy shook his head, sobbing. "Mẹ..."

She hugged him fiercely, kissed his forehead, and memorized the weight of him. Then she pushed him gently toward May. May hesitated. It felt wrong and unnatural to tear a child from his mother. But Mrs. Tran's eyes said everything. There was no choice. With trembling hands, May took Duy and guided him to the car.

Mrs. Tran stepped back. "Go. Before it's too late." Duy screamed. He thrashed, clawing to escape, reaching for her. "MẸ!" It wasn't just a word. It was a wound.

Mrs. Tran covered her mouth, shaking. She didn't run. She couldn't. She just stood there, watching, as the little olive drab car, dark and lightless, rolled away into the night. Duy's tear-streaked face pressed against the rear window, his small hand reaching back until the shadows swallowed his mother whole. No headlights. No hesitation.

The road ahead stretched like a cracked ribbon into nothingness. Behind them, war was no longer distant. Gunfire snapped. Explosions thumped. The earth itself seemed to flinch. The Beetle's engine hummed like a desperate prayer. In the rearview mirror, smoke consumed the stars. There was no map. No plan. Only the road, and it was vanishing fast.

Chapter 4

Arriving in the Fishing Village

By the time they reached Quang's house, about 45 minutes south of Vĩnh Long, in the quiet countryside of Bình Minh, the village was already deserted. The roads had narrowed to gravel, lined with swaying coconut palms in the thick night air. Insects buzzed steadily in the trees, their chorus undisturbed by any sign of human life. Even Quang Minh's old military friend and fellow deserter was gone. The house stood silent, hollowed of life

Inside the small wooden home, the air was heavy with dust and stillness. On the rough kitchen table lay a folded sheet of paper, its creases soft from repeated handling. Minh picked it up and immediately recognized Quang's careful handwriting: My dear brother, I couldn't stay any longer. I'm sorry I had to leave before you.

In the shack, there's a boat hidden, ready. Please take it. Save your family. I pray you all make it out safely. May

15

Heaven protect you. I hope we meet again, in freedom or the next life.

Minh stared at the note for a long time, the words swimming before his eyes. A lump formed in his throat. He hadn't seen Quang in days, but their bond, shaped by survival and war, had never weakened. Now, even that thread had vanished into the night. He thought of the barracks, of Quang's easy laugh as he told stories about childhood pranks and lost loves. Those moments of levity had been rare lifelines in a collapsing world. They had made a promise to each other: if it ever came to this, they would protect one another's families. Quang had kept his promise.

The village was ghostly. Minh stepped out into the moonlit street, searching for any sign of life. But every house was dark. Fires were cold. Laundry hung stiff on the lines. Doors creaked open in the wind. Everyone had fled, leaving only fragments behind scattered belongings, a child's sandal, a toppled bicycle. The stillness pressed in on him. Then he saw it a small shack near the bend of the river.

Inside, beneath a canvas tarp, was the boat Quang had promised: a weathered fishing vessel, its wooden sides chipped and peeling. Minh approached cautiously, heart pounding. He climbed in and checked the engine, which was rusted but intact. Gritting his teeth, he turned the key. The engine coughed, sputtered, then roared to life with a mechanical groan. The sound echoed down the river.

"Hoang!" Minh shouted, breaking the silence. "We need gasoline check the shack, the house, anywhere! Search the whole village if you have to! Siphon whatever's left from the cars!" Hoang didn't hesitate. He darted off, slipping through doorways, digging through shadows. Minutes later, he returned sweaty, scraped, and breathless with three nearly empty fuel cans. It wasn't much, but it was something. His arms were oil-streaked, his hands raw, as he handed them over.

Minh's hands trembled as he poured the fuel into the tank. Every creak, every gust of wind sounded sharper now. He glanced back at the silent village, every shadow a possible threat. "Chi, Khanh, Phuong, grab everything from the car," he called. "Load it onto the boat." The children moved quickly, arms full of blankets, food, and the last of their belongings. May stood nearby, holding baby Ngoc tightly, her eyes flicking between her children and the jungle beyond. Her chest rose and fell rapidly, not from exertion, but from fear.

Minh moved with urgency, draping tarps over the younger children to shield them from the rain and prying eyes. "Get in," he said. His voice was steady but edged with tension. They climbed aboard. Trong whimpered, clutching May's áo bà ba (Traditional Vietnamese garment). Duy sat silently, his face blank, still reeling from the pain of leaving his mother behind. The boat rocked gently as the children settled in, filling every inch of space. Minh gave one last look at the riverbank, then pushed them off.

The river accepted them with quiet indifference. Its wide, glassy surface reflected a moon half-hidden by clouds. They drifted slowly, the boat's motor humming low, the only other sounds the gentle splash of paddles and the hum of crickets. Each child breathed in shallow gulps, afraid that even a sigh might give them away. Chi kept a hand on Sang's back, wordlessly soothing her. Then came the shouting.

Voices rose from the riverbank, cracking through the night like gunfire. Minh's head jerked up. Dark shapes emerged, North Vietnamese soldiers, rifles slung over their shoulders. "Down!" he hissed. "Everyone lie flat!" The children obeyed instantly, ducking beneath the tarps. May froze at the bow, her nón lá (Vietnamese conical hat) tilted low over her face. Her breath came shallow. Her body trembled. She held Ngoc tighter, the baby still asleep in her arms.

"Who are you?!" the soldiers barked, their voices in unison guttural, harsh, and commanding. The question was

18

no question at all. It was a warning. The sound sliced through the humid air like a blade. Minh's heart seized. Panic, sharp, cold, rose in his chest. For one terrifying moment, he froze. Just one heartbeat. But instinct took over. He stepped forward, snapping to attention with his spine straight. His voice rose, controlled and sharp, mimicking a Northern officer's clipped cadence.

"We're supply runners!" he called back. The words rang out with practiced authority. He had erased every trace of his Southern accent, wrapping his words in the cold tone he'd heard daily from enemy commanders and once joked about with friends in fleeting moments of calm. But this wasn't a game. This was survival. His mouth was dry, his tongue thick. Still, he pushed the words out, praying the fear in his gut wouldn't reach his throat.

"From where?" a soldier demanded. A flashlight beam cut across the water wide, blinding, scanning for lies. "Unit 32, out of Phú Thọ sector," Minh said instantly. The lie formed fast, pulled from memory. He had once operated near there. He knew the structure, the routine, the language. Now, that buried knowledge rose like a lifeline. "What's the password for tonight?"

Minh's stomach dropped a cold, sickening plunge, but only for a split second, barely a hiccup in his carefully held composure. He knew the soldiers rotated passwords often. A security precaution. He had no idea what tonight's was. Still, he took the gamble. "Lantern," he said, his voice steady, betraying none of the turmoil tightening his chest. A tense silence followed. One of the soldiers muttered something to another low, unintelligible but heavy with meaning. The pause stretched, taut as wire.

Then, at last, a gruff voice barked from the bank: "You're late." Minh let out a slow breath controlled, quiet, just enough to reply without seeming relieved. "Engine trouble," he said calmly. "Current's rough tonight." Another silence fell longer, heavier. May crouched low behind him, holding her breath. The humid air felt suddenly still, like the jungle itself had gone silent, pressing down on them from all sides. Finally, one soldier called out, his voice sharp and final: "Move along. Make it quick." The figures faded into the darkness, swallowed by the night.

Minh stood frozen a moment longer, every nerve on edge, before turning slowly back to the boat. May didn't look up her gaze fixed on the black water but he saw her shoulders sink, just slightly. A single, almost invisible shiver passed through her body. It said everything. The silence returned thick, immense, suffocating. Every soft splash of water, every insect hum from the reeds, now sounded unnaturally loud. The river held them in limbo, each heartbeat waiting for the next sound: a gunshot... or the fragile blessing of peace.

Chapter 5

Adrift on the Open Sea

They had just left the river behind, its winding, familiar current giving way to the open sea. Now the water stretched endlessly in every direction, an unforgiving expanse beneath a starless sky. Waves lifted their small fishing boat like a toy and dropped it again, over and over, as if the sea itself were testing their will. Below deck, the engine rattled with effort, growling through each turn of its aging gears.

Some of the younger children had fallen asleep, curled against their siblings, lulled by the rhythm of the waves and the quiet weight of exhaustion. Others sat wide-eyed, staring into the void that had swallowed the world around them. No lights. No horizon. Only blackness and the low hum of dread. They huddled together, silent, shoulder to shoulder, holding onto hope like a fraying thread.

May sat near the stern, cradling Trong against her chest. He was warm but alarmingly thin, his breath shallow as he slept. She could feel every rib, every delicate bone, as if he were made of little more than air and willpower. Shifting slightly, she adjusted her áo bà ba (traditional outfit) to shield his face from the wind. In the stillness, May's thoughts wandered back to another escape, long ago.

She had been just a girl in 1954 when the French fell at Điện Biên Phủ. The mountains turned red with blood. Artillery thundered for days. She remembered the tremors in the ground, the grown men sobbing openly. When the noise stopped, silence followed, but it was not peace. It was dread. Her mother had woken her before dawn. They left without a sound, carrying only what they could hide beneath their áo dài. May remembered the silence of the land, as if even the trees were holding their breath. Still, they had stayed in Vietnam. Even then, they believed something was left to hold onto.

Now, she sat adrift with her own children, leaving behind not just a war, but the country itself. The land behind them was no longer home. The one ahead is a mystery. The salt wind stung her skin. She blinked back tears and pulled Trong closer. When he sank into deeper sleep, she passed him gently to Chi, who reached out with trembling arms. May then gathered baby Ngoc into her lap and curled around her, shielding her from the spray. She sang softly old lullabies from her village, songs passed from mother to daughter, as steady as breath.

Around her neck, the jade pendant still hung: a green lotus blossom carved into stone, tied to a faded silk cord. Her mother had fastened it there the night they first ran. "For luck," she had whispered. "For remembering." May touched it now, her fingers closing tightly around it. It had survived everything. She wondered if it still held power.

The sea groaned beneath them. Above, clouds swallowed the moon, leaving only the occasional flicker of starlight. Their boat creaked with age and strain. Once it had carried fish, tools, and stories. Now it carried something else: escape, desperation, and everything they still dared to dream. Minh sat at the bow, hunched forward, arms resting on his knees. His eyes were bloodshot with fatigue. Beside him, Hoang watched the sputtering engine. "It won't last," Minh said quietly, just loud enough for Hoang to hear. "Fuel's low. Current's stronger out here." "We'll float," Hoang replied. "The sea is wide."

"But floating's not living," Minh murmured. "We need direction. A ship. Or a miracle." Then came a gasp. "Anh!" Long cried, pointing ahead. "Look! A ship!" Everyone turned, breath caught in their throats. May's head snapped up. Her arms tightened protectively around Ngoc.

For a moment, there was only fog and sea and doubt. And then emerging from the mist, a dark shape. Large. Steady. Too massive, too deliberate, to be just another fishing vessel. A chill passed through them, sharp and sudden.

The older children leaned forward instinctively, eyes wide with shared apprehension. "Is it a patrol?" Chi whispered, her voice barely more than breath thin, uncertain, and edged with dread. Minh rose slowly, his figure tall and rigid against the pale light of dawn. He stared at the approaching vessel, unmoving. After a long, tense pause, he said quietly, "No. That's not one of ours." A fragile thread of hope began to unfurl across the boat, tentative, almost too delicate to name. "Is it Navy?" someone whispered.

May said nothing. Her gaze stayed locked on the ship, growing larger with every heartbeat. Her chest pounded, and her mother's pendant gripped tightly in her hand. The jade stone felt strangely warm against her skin. Around her, the children watched silently, waiting, looking to her not for answers, but for strength. Duy clutched the boat's edge and whispered, "Please… let them see us." Still, the ship drew closer slowly, steadily, parting the sea like something out of a dream. They waited. They hoped. And in that suspended space between silence and rescue, between

the country behind them and the unknown ahead, they dared
for the first time in days to believe

Chapter 6

The Climb to Salvation

A colossal shadow emerged on the horizon, swelling slowly in the pale pre-dawn light. It consumed the dim sky as it drew nearer, a silent leviathan cutting through the restless sea. The vessel moved with quiet, unshakable authority, its iron hull weathered and scarred, bearing the marks of storms, distance, and time. From the mist-shrouded water, it rose like an ancient titan, relentless and immense. Its approach was deliberate, agonizingly slow, yet utterly inevitable like fate itself closing in, pulling them closer with every frantic heartbeat.

Minh's small, battered fishing boat scraped against the cargo ship's rust-streaked hull, the jolt echoing like a warning bell. High above, a rope ladder, a crude Lotsenleiter, swayed in the wind. Frayed and salt-crusted, its ends dipped into the churning seafoam. It was their only way up. Their only chance. May's breath came in short, sharp gasps, each inhale scraped raw by fear. In the distance, other small boats emerged as shadows against the brightening sky, darting toward the ship with the same desperate hope. But time was vanishing. Behind them, a darker shadow crawled along the horizon, a silent, looming threat. There was no time left to think.

May moved quickly, her trembling fingers guided by instinct. She laid a worn cloth on the damp floor, its familiar texture grounding her. With careful hands, she placed baby Ngoc in its center and wrapped her tightly, binding her to her chest. The infant whimpered once, then settled, soothed by her mother's warmth and heartbeat. Without hesitation, May turned to the rope ladder, now swinging wildly in the wind. She seized the first wet rung, her muscles burning from the weight of her child, of fear, of everything they carried. The rough rope bit into her hands, but she didn't falter. She couldn't.

Above her, the massive ship loomed as a cold promise of safety. Below, the sea thrashed like a living thing. Between them, suspended in terror and hope, May climbed. A wave slammed into the boat, a wall of green that rocked them violently. The impact sent a shockwave through the ladder. Minh clutched the bottom rung with one hand and gripped the boat's edge with the other. "Go! Now!" he shouted, his voice hoarse over the roar of the sea. May looked up. The ladder twisted and lurched with every swell. Figures leaned over the railing above. "More down there!" someone shouted in Lao, the voice sharp with command. Then, in broken Vietnamese, another man cried out, "Next one climb! Hurry!"

Hands reached down, motioning frantically. The ladder seemed impossibly thin, just a thread between drowning and survival. Could she do this? She had to. May gritted her teeth and reached again. Her hands ached, her arms on fire, but she pulled herself upward. One rung. Then another. The wind lashed her face. Salt stung her eyes. The ladder swung, jerking unpredictably with the waves. A man above leaned dangerously far over the rail, clutching the rope with white-knuckled fists. His voice tore through the wind: "Don't look down! Don't look down!" He repeated it over and over, his words a lifeline thrown through the storm. His face was drawn with urgency, his eyes locked on hers, willing her to climb, to survive.

Below, in the pitching boat, Khanh crouched low, her small body trembling uncontrollably. A cold dread crept up through the damp wood beneath her and into her bones, chilling her to the core. Her wide, terrified eyes never left her mother, who was inching slowly, agonizingly up the swaying rope ladder dangling from the cargo ship's towering side. Strapped tightly to her mother's chest, bundled in a thin, worn blanket, was Khanh's baby sister, Ngoc, so small, so still. The ladder lurched with every gust of wind, every heave of the merciless sea. Khanh clung to the edge of the boat, her knuckles bone-white, her breath shallow and fast. She hovered between paralyzing panic and a silent, desperate prayer.

Every groan of the rope sounded like a scream. Her heartbeat thudded louder than the crashing waves, a frantic drumbeat in her ears. What if the ladder broke? What if her mother fell? What if the sea swallowed them whole? The thoughts came fast and sharp, each one a blow that knocked the air from her lungs. And still she stared, her gaze locked on the bundle strapped to her mother's chest, so still, so impossibly fragile. Far too small for a world this violent, this indifferent. The wind clawed at her mother's coat, at the blanket, at the rope. Everything felt too thin, too breakable. The ocean below looked like a monster, vast and waiting, mouth wide open.

Khanh hugged her knees to her chest, rocking with the motion of the boat, her body a coil of terror. She couldn't scream. Couldn't cry. She just watched, paralyzed, as the two people she loved most dangled above the endless, hungry sea. One more step. Then another. May's entire body ached. Every muscle burned. But then hands. Strong hands. Reaching. Grasping under her arms and pulling her over the railing. She collapsed onto the steel deck, gasping, her limbs shaking. Around her, voices shouted, boots pounded the deck, and chaos churned. But May focused only on the bundle pressed against her chest.

Frantically, she loosened the blanket, fingers fumbling. Ngoc's chest moved, rising and falling. A small, shallow breath. Alive. Safe. But Chi was still climbing. May staggered to her feet, legs weak and unsteady, and rushed to the rail. Her breath caught as she spotted her daughter still clinging to the ladder, face pale, eyes wide with fear, fingers wrapped tight around the wet rope. And then she looked up. A wave. Towering. Impossibly vast. Charging forward like a liquid wall. A crushing weight sank into May's chest. Her breath vanished. Chi was trapped midway up the ladder, exposed, vulnerable.

May's limbs froze. She wanted to scream, to run, to reach her child, but panic held her like a vise. The image of Chi slipping, vanishing into the black sea, was unbearable. Her heart thundered. The roar filled her ears, drowning everything else. The world shrank to just Chi and the wave. And May could only watch, helpless, as time ran out.

31

At that moment, a second small boat, its hull weathered but sturdy, pulled alongside Minh's, bumping gently against its side. Onboard were several older passengers, their faces marked by fatigue and hardship, but their spirits unbroken. Among them was a young man whose sharp eyes quickly scanned the chaotic scene above. Without speaking, he eased his boat closer, matching its rhythm with Minh's. The contact between hulls spoke of silent agreement, a shared desperation, a mutual resolve. The young man didn't hesitate.

With the grace of an athlete, he leapt onto the rope ladder. The sudden jolt nearly ripped it from Chi's hands. She cried out a sharp, terrified yelp as the ladder swayed violently. Her fingers clenched tighter, knuckles whitening, fighting to hold on. But the man was already climbing. Smooth, confident, focused. One hand reached back to her, a steady touch in the storm. "It's okay," he said gently in Vietnamese. His voice was low, calm, and an anchor in the chaos. "I have you." With reassuring care, he guided her upward, his strong hands bracing each of her trembling steps. At the top, crew members waited with grim, focused expressions, ready to pull her to safety. As soon as Chi was aboard, the young man turned and began climbing down again without pause, without fanfare.

A silent, unwavering presence. One by one, he reached for each child still below. His eyes, intense and warm, met theirs with quiet encouragement. His voice, calm and steady, cut through their fear. "You're safe. Just take my hand." At first, they hesitated. Then, slowly, trust broke through. Small hands reached for his, and together they climbed. He helped each child with unwavering focus, steady hands, patient words, and endless care. He paused only long enough to ensure each one was safely aboard before turning back again. His movements were a blur of precision. His gaze never left the sea, constantly scanning always ready.

Meanwhile, Minh worked quickly to lash their boat to the massive ship. The ropes groaned under tension, but held fast. As the last of the children ascended, Minh looked up. He and the young man locked eyes for a moment. Minh gave a single nod. Respect. Gratitude. Understanding. The danger wasn't gone. The sea still churned, the storm still threatened. But something had shifted. In place of panic was resolve in place of isolation, teamwork. Above, the waves slapped gently at the hull. The ropes strained and creaked. But a fragile bubble of hope had begun to rise, held aloft by trust, quiet courage, and the tireless coordination of two men who had never met, but who now stood together between chaos and survival.

Chapter 7

Ensured Fair Food Distribution

The old rescue ship was no gleaming beacon of hope, it was a rusted freighter, its massive hull weathered by years of battling the sea's brutal temperament. Thick scabs of rust mottled the surface, brown and black like old wounds, while clusters of barnacles clung to its pitted sides like ancient parasites. The deck, once bustling, was now a chaotic sprawl of corroded machinery, tangled cables, and tattered life rafts whose orange fabric had faded to a ghostly pallor. The superstructure, intended for command, was reduced to exposed metal and fogged windows; the bridge was silent and seemingly abandoned. The ship felt less like salvation than a floating prison.

The captain was no man of epaulets and polished brass. He wore practical, worn clothing that mirrored the rough, honest life he'd lived along Vietnam's demanding coast. His calloused hands bore the marks of years navigating treacherous waters and bustling ports. Though the ship was designed to transport cargo, not people, his deep humanity overruled practicality. He hadn't planned to flee his homeland, but as Vietnam's crisis deepened, something within him shifted. He knew he had to act. Respected deeply by his crew, he was known not just for his skill but for his fairness and compassion. While the crew was used to hard labor, they trusted him implicitly. The cargo ship, once built for goods, had become a lifeline, unexpected, imperfect, but vital. He was seen by many as a quiet protector, even a hero.

From the moment their feet touched the cold steel deck, May felt a shift in the air, a collective unease. Relief from escaping the open sea was real, but it was quickly replaced by something heavier: uncertainty. Claustrophobia. For the first few hours, everything was surreal. The ship's crew moved through the crowd efficiently, handing out thin blankets and small cups of water, mostly to wide-eyed children. But the reality soon settled in: this was not the haven they had imagined. The decks were overcrowded, the air stifling, every inch claimed. Hope gave way to tension, thick and unyielding. As the ship drifted into calmer waters, the divide among passengers grew more visible.

A small group stood apart, those with wealth and foresight. They wore clean clothes, sat comfortably on mats or stools, and brought bulging bags filled with private food supplies. They ate openly, with casual indifference, while others crouched nearby with nothing, parched, starving, watching in silence. These fortunate few didn't offer help. They didn't even acknowledge the suffering just feet away. May watched with a tight, burning discomfort as children, some younger than hers, cried quietly, hollow-eyed. She had nothing but a damp bundle of clothes, a few tarnished coins, and a mother's instinct to put her children first. Her hunger clawed at her, but she refused to eat until her children were safe. Around her, others looked just as frail. May knew many hadn't eaten in days.

The tension rose like a brewing storm. A skeletal woman stood with her eyes fixed on the wealthy group, on their fruit, their bread, the grilled meat. Her hunger wasn't just physical. It was moral. It was the rage of someone who had lost too much and still had to watch others hoard what could save lives. Then the captain stepped forward. His quiet authority parted the crowd. He stood in the center of the deck, and his voice cut through the restless murmurs.

"We cannot go on like this," he said. "The food must be shared. All food and drink will be collected and distributed equally among participants. Everyone deserves to eat." There were murmurs, some hopeful, others angry. One woman in a silk blouse, clearly from the wealthy group, rose with disdain etched across her face. "I'm not giving my food away," she said coldly. "It's mine. You can't force me." May stared, stunned. This woman had everything. And yet, she clung to it while children starved.

Before things could escalate, a young man, the same one who had helped May's child onto the ship, stopped forward. His presence was quiet but sharp. He walked up to the woman without a word. His eyes met hers, then dropped to the bag clutched to her chest. "Your food will be shared," he said. She gasped and tried to pull away, but he was quicker. He took the bag, firm but calm, revealing bread, dried fish, and canned goods, enough to feed a dozen families. Her scream of protest was lost in the growing murmur of the crowd. Approval surged.

The bag was handed to a crew member and carried away. The woman, red with fury, didn't speak again. The young man glanced at May, just briefly. His eyes, which had been hard a moment ago, softened. And then he turned and disappeared into the crowd. The captain gave another order. The crew, now with full authority, gathered supplies and began distributing food fairly. May received a steaming bowl of rice and a few boiled vegetables. Her stomach twisted painfully, but the food was only part of what filled her there was also bitterness. The unfairness of the world.

38

The cruelty that lived alongside survival. Then Trong tugged at her sleeve. His face was dirty and tired, but his eyes still held hope. For him for her children she would keep going.

She ate. Not because the food was enough. Not because it gave her strength or satisfaction. She ate because she had to. Everyone aboard did. Each bite was survival, not comfort, and the act of swallowing became an unspoken pact to keep living a little longer. The ship had not been built for this, for hundreds of men, women, and children pressed together on its tired deck. It was made to carry cargo, not 375 souls fleeing with nothing but fear in their bones and hope in their hearts. Every creak of the planks, every groan of the steel, seemed to remind them of their fragility. The vessel sagged under the human weight, its joints straining like tired lungs gasping for air.

For two brutal days, the sea tossed them as if they were nothing more than driftwood. Waves slammed against the hull, spraying salt that stung the eyes and burned the lips of already parched mouths. Children whimpered in their mothers' arms, too weak to cry fully, their voices reduced to small whines lost in the roar of water. Men tried to steady the boat, though their arms trembled from exhaustion.

Then, as if nature itself had paused, the waters calmed. The endless grey horizon softened. The sea lay still. Someone spotted it first, a thin strip of dark rising above the waterline. A whisper traveled across the crowded deck. The word spread like a spark leaping from one mouth to another. Thailand. Land. For a heartbeat, time slowed. Faces lifted from their despair. Spines straightened. The air changed. Hope, fragile but alive, rippled through the crowd like a breeze through dry grass. Mothers kissed their children's heads, whispering promises of safety. Men closed their eyes in silent prayers.

And then came the sound. Low, mechanical, steady. Engines. The air vibrated before the sight revealed itself. Two patrol boats cut through the water, their white wakes slicing toward the refugee ship with the precision of predators closing in on wounded prey. They circled deliberately, tightening the ring, the dark hulls glistening in the light. On their decks stood armed men in pressed uniforms. Their weapons hung ready. Their faces gave nothing away.

A crackle broke through the air as a loudspeaker came alive. The voice that followed was sharp, metallic, and final.

"Do not enter Thai waters. Leave now."

The words struck like a whip. They bounced against the metal hull and echoed into every chest. Mothers clutched their children tighter. A hush fell over the deck as eyes darted from the patrol boats to the coastline, so close yet already slipping away.

The loudspeaker came again, the same voice, clipped and mechanical. "Return to sea immediately. This coast is closed. Turn around."

It did not sound like a warning. It sounded like a verdict already passed down. The officer's voice was cold, a sound drained of any trace of compassion. The message came again, louder now, as if volume could erase humanity.

"You are not allowed to land. Turn around now."

The words tore through the fragile fabric of hope. Some gasped, others shook their heads in disbelief. Murmurs swelled into cries. A woman dropped to her knees, her body convulsing with sobs that would not stop. A man raised both hands high, his palms spread open toward the soldiers as if he were offering his very life in exchange for mercy. Desperate voices called out in broken Thai, in English, in Vietnamese. Each plea tumbled into the sea, unanswered.

What none of them understood fully in that moment was that Thailand had already closed its borders by land and sea. The refugee camps were full to bursting. The people were weary of strangers. The government was unwilling to shoulder another burden. To the patrols, the refugees were no longer human lives to be saved, but numbers, an endless tide threatening to drown their shores. Thailand was finished.

He stood at the edge of the deck, a weathered man with sunken eyes who had watched too many waves of rejection already. He did not curse. He did not plead. His hands gripped the megaphone so tightly his knuckles whitened, but his face betrayed no fear. He looked carved from the sea itself, hard and immovable. When he spoke, his voice carried over the stunned silence with a clarity that cut through grief.

"This ship will not dock in Thailand. We are heading to Malaysia."

The crowd erupted. Cries of protest rose, desperate, furious voices overlapping in disbelief. Fists lifted. People begged, shouted, and demanded answers. But then, as if the last reserves of energy had drained from them all at once, the noise died. A heavy silence settled over the ship, thicker than the heat. Minh froze, standing beside his younger siblings, his face drained of color. May's lips trembled. "No… no," she whispered, her breath catching in her throat. The word felt like a plea tossed into a void. A mother nearby broke into sobs, clutching her baby as if she could block out the truth with the force of her arms. Others sank to the steel floor, eyes vacant, hope slipping from their hands like sand.

Minh turned to May. "What now?" he asked, his voice barely audible. May didn't respond at first. Her eyes stared out at the hazy horizon, where Thailand had vanished like a broken promise. Her throat ached with the weight of it. Then she spoke, quiet, but unshaken. "We live," she said. "Even if the world turns its back, we live." And the ship groaned forward, its engines grinding toward Malaysia, into the wide, terrifying unknown. There were 375 people crammed onto the boat, a human mosaic of desperation. Most sat with knees pulled tightly to their chests for nearly seven grueling days. There was no room to stretch, no space to lie flat. They pressed against strangers, skin to skin, enduring suffocating days and freezing, exposed nights. The air stank, sweat, stale urine, and the dense, sour smell of fear.

April's days had been hot, humid, and mercifully calm. But now it was May. The Southwest Monsoon had come. Stronger winds. Unforgiving rains. A once-passable sea became a violent, churning beast. On the second night, the storm arrived. The waves rose like black mountains, towering and crashing down with wrath. The ship rocked like a child's toy tossed in a bathtub. People screamed, their voices no match for the wind. They prayed, whispers, sobs, pleas to any god willing to hear. They clung to one another with everything they had.

May held Trong and Ngoc with all her strength, her arms locked tight. Trong trembled violently, his breathing shallow and quick. She pressed him to her chest, whispering into his ear, fierce and raw: "Hold on. Stay with me. Don't let go." The older children wrapped themselves around the younger ones, their bodies shields against the madness

44

outside. Freezing saltwater crashed into them, searing their eyes, choking their throats. The rain fell in sheets, hard and endless. The wind screamed through the night like a living thing. Lightning tore the sky in flashes, casting eerie glimpses of huddled, shaking forms. Still, they held on.

The sea could roar. The storm could rage. But they would not let go. The deck became a grotesque tableau of human misery. People retched violently, their bodies convulsing as they emptied themselves into the swirling tide of vomit and seawater. The ship's relentless lurching twisted every stomach into agony, each heave a desperate rhythm against the storm's roar. The acrid stench of bile mixed with the sharp tang of salt air, forming a putrid haze that clung to every breath, a searing reminder of their helplessness.

The sick lay sprawled and ignored, their cries lost to the wind. The dead, stiffening in the open, could not be mourned. Their stillness became a silent, chilling burden. People sat, crouched, or collapsed in their filth, the bile of their suffering soaked into their clothes and skin. There was no escape. No comfort. Only the raw, endless torment of survival. When the storm finally broke, the morning was eerily quiet. The humid air had lifted, a small mercy, but nothing else had changed for the better. The sky, now pale and bleached, gave way to a dull sun veiled in haze. The sea had stilled, flat and glassy, mirroring the light in a way that felt more like a trick than a reprieve. The scent of salt, dampness, and something metallic still hung in the air. Rainwater pooled in the corners of the deck. Blankets and clothes lay soaked, limp reminders of the night before.

But the silence held no peace. The ship's fuel was nearly gone. Supplies were down to scraps. The captain stood alone at the helm, staring toward the horizon with hollow eyes. He said nothing, but the truth was clear: Malaysia, their final hope, was still a full day away. May and her children clung to each other, bodies weak, hearts thinned by fear and exhaustion. They had been changed. Not just worn down, but reshaped by what they had endured. They couldn't look to the sky for comfort. The heavens were as blank and silent as the sea below, vast, uncaring, infinite. They were drifting, unseen and unwanted, in a world with no place for them.

All they had was each other. And that last flicker of hope. That they would survive.

Chapter 8

Arriving at Bidong Island, Malaysia

Day after day, the tropical sun scorched their skin without mercy, turning the freighter's deck into a blistering griddle. The turquoise sea shimmered like polished glass, dazzling, indifferent. At night, the temperature dropped. Damp salt stiffened their clothes, and the humid heat gave way to biting cold. They lay huddled together, trembling beneath a canopy of stars that offered no warmth, only silence. They were sunburned, dehydrated, hollowed out by the endless days at sea. Hope unraveled with each passing wave, until suddenly, the wind shifted.

A new scent drifted on the breeze: damp, earthy land. A gull cried overhead. Then another. Seabirds. People surged to the railings, eyes scanning the horizon. At first, there was nothing. Then, slowly, a smudge appeared, green, solid, real. Someone shouted, and the cry rippled through the crowd: "Land!" The boat slowed. The freighter creaked and groaned as if exhausted by the journey. But the voices

47

aboard surged with cautious awe. It was Bidong Island. They had arrived.

When May stepped onto the sand, her knees nearly gave out. The earth was soft, too soft after days of steel and rocking water. Around her, others fell to their knees and kissed the ground, whispering prayers of thanks. The island, ringed by dense jungle, was beautiful in its wildness, but eerily still, the silence broken only by the murmurs of hundreds of others like them. It was May 1975. Pulau Bidong, once a quiet, uninhabited island in the South China Sea, had become an accidental haven. There were no barracks, no fences, only open beaches, tangled trees, and the exhausted.

Refugees built makeshift shelters from bamboo poles, fishing nets, and sails torn from boats. Fires crackled near the tree line. People scavenged for coconuts and caught rainwater in cans and broken jugs. At night, the island echoed with soft cries of the sick and the haunted silence of those mourning the lost. May held her children close as UN officials arrived, taking names, issuing numbers, handing out thin blankets and ration kits. Aid groups followed: the Red Cross, Red Crescent, doctors from Europe, and Canada. They brought medicine, soft-spoken translators, and clipped voices trying to soothe. But the island was overwhelmed. Disease spread fast. Food was never enough.

Local fishermen brought rice and water. Some villagers whispered prayers and left behind tarps, pots, and kindness. And still, the boats kept coming. Hundreds. Then thousands. May saw familiar faces from Saigon, a schoolteacher, a fruit vendor, a soldier who once bought pastries for his daughter. They arrived barefoot and broken, asking the same questions she had whispered only days before. Minh and Hoang helped bury an older man who died the first night. No one knew his name. No one had the strength to shed a tear. Immigration officials came from France, Germany, Canada, and Australia. They carried clipboards and asked:

Where are you from? Do you have family abroad? Are you willing to resettle? May answered carefully. She spoke of her husband. Her children. Her promise. "We will go to America," she said. "Only America." The officials nodded, but said nothing. By the end of 1975, Bidong had become a refugee camp in name, if not yet in structure. Thousands lived in tents and patched huts of plastic and wood. Children played with driftwood and empty cans. They had nothing, but they survived because they refused to give up. At night, May sat with her children around a cooking fire.

She boiled rice, told stories, not of war, but of spring flowers, her mother's soup, and kites over the rooftops of Saigon. And sometimes, just before sleep, she stood alone on the sand, watching the sea. Not for the past. But for the ship that would come.

Chapter 9

The Fever That Wouldn't Break

For six months now, May's family had called the refugee camp in Malaysia home. Though it was safer than the chaos they'd fled, life here was a daily struggle, crowded tents, long food lines, and the relentless heat pressing down on the thousands of displaced souls in this limbo. Makeshift shelters stretched in endless rows, their canvas walls offering little privacy. The air was thick with the scent of seawater and damp earth, mingling with the aroma of rice and fish from the communal kitchens. Each morning, May woke to the sounds of murmured prayers, crying children, and the distant blare of a ship's horn in the harbor.

Ships arrived from every corner of the world, including Japan, Singapore, Canada, Australia, and distant European countries such as Germany, the UK, and France. They brought supplies, medical aid, and most importantly, hope. Some lucky families would hear their names called, their paperwork approved, and board these ships bound for an unknown but long-awaited freedom. But for May's family, the wait dragged on. And then came the fever. At first, it seemed like exhaustion. Phuong complained of headaches and skipped meals. Her usual chatter was missing. By the fourth day, she couldn't sit up. Her skin burned with fever.

When May touched her daughter's forehead, she jerked her hand back, it was like touching boiling water. "Phuong?" she whispered, leaning in. "Con ơi, wake up." There was only a faint, muffled moan. Her other children gathered around, fear written across their faces. Hoang knelt beside his sister. Long clung to May's skirt. Minh hovered nearby, eyes wide and silent. "She's burning up," May said. "She hasn't eaten in three days. She can barely breathe." Minh didn't hesitate. He stepped outside the tent and walked, fast, purposeful, toward the Red Cross station.

The clinic stood at the heart of the camp: a rectangular tent with two benches and a faded flag hanging limp above the entrance. Refugees waited in haphazard lines. Volunteers moved in and out with clipboards and supply boxes. Inside, doctors and nurses battled an avalanche of emergencies with a fraction of what they needed. Minh pushed forward, his heart thudding. "I need a doctor," he told the man at the folding table. "My sister's very sick." The man barely looked up. "Name?"

"She's not on a list. But she has a high fever, four days now. She won't eat. She's shaking. There's a rash. Please." "No voucher?" "No." "Then come back when she's worse." Minh's face flushed. "If I wait, she'll die." Someone muttered behind him, "We all have sick children. What makes yours different?" Minh turned. "I don't know. Nothing. But she's my sister."

Just then, a young Vietnamese doctor paused near the tent flap. He had a stethoscope around his neck, a pen tucked behind one ear, and deep shadows under his eyes. He glanced over, only half-interested. Minh stepped toward him. "Please," he said, voice breaking. "Just look at her. If you think she's fine, I won't ask again." The doctor hesitated. "Symptoms?" "High fever. No food or water. Rash on her stomach. She can barely speak." His eyebrows rose. "A rash?" Minh nodded. The doctor sighed. "I'm not supposed to leave... but if that's typhoid, she may not have time." He turned to a nurse. "Cover me for fifteen minutes."

Then to Minh: "Show me." Minh didn't reply. He just ran. Back at the tent, May knelt beside Phuong, wiping her face with a damp cloth. Chi sat outside sharpening her knife, though her eyes never left the flap. When Minh

53

returned, breathless and trailed by the doctor, everyone stepped aside. The doctor knelt quickly, checking Phuong's pulse, breathing, and tongue. Then he sat back. "It's typhoid fever," he said. May closed her eyes. Chi exhaled slowly. "Typhoid?" Hoang asked.

The doctor nodded. "It's a bacterial infection, probably from contaminated food or water. It starts slow but turns dangerous fast. She's already severely dehydrated. Her fever's over 104. Without antibiotics, she won't survive the week." He paused, glancing toward Phuong's motionless form on the cot, her chest rising and falling in shallow, rapid breaths. If the fever doesn't break soon...", he hesitated, choosing his words carefully, "there could be permanent damage. The brain doesn't always walk away unscathed after a fever this high for so long. Even if she survives, she may not be the same. She may experience difficulties with memory, speech, or movement. We'll do everything we can, but you need to be prepared."

"Can you give her something?" May asked. The doctor looked away. "I wish I could. I'd give it myself. But it's all locked. Rationed. The last course went to a child leaving tomorrow." "There's nothing?" Minh asked. He stood up. "Nothing official. But some nurses keep private supplies. I'll ask tonight." He turned to May. "You've done everything right. Keep cooling her. If you find coconut water or broth, give her small sips. If we can get antibiotics soon, she still has a real chance." He paused at the flap of the tent, his voice dropping to a near whisper.

"I wasn't supposed to come," he admitted softly. "But you made me. And I'm glad I did."

A few hours later, when the camp had quieted into uneasy sleep, a gentle knock tapped against the wooden post of their shelter. The sound was cautious, almost secretive. The doctor slipped inside, his figure little more than a shadow against the dim light, his voice low and urgent.

"I found someone," he said. "A nurse. Filipino. She has a stash."

May rose instantly, hope flickering in her eyes as she searched his face. "Will she give it to us?"

He hesitated, his breath catching. "She said yes... if we can offer her something in return."

Minh's jaw tightened, "We have nothing."

The air thickened, silence pressing down like a weight. Then the doctor slowly lowered himself to the floor. From his worn leather bag, he drew out two weathered metal tags. The edges were dulled with time, but the names etched into them still glimmered faintly in the lantern light. He cradled them in his hands as if they were made of stone and memory.

"She'll get these," he said quietly. "One carries my name. The other, my father's. They're all I have left of him… and of myself. But I'd rather give them up than watch your daughter die."

May pressed a hand to her chest, speechless. Wrapped in wax paper were eight small white pills, chloramphenicol. Precious. Rare. Life-saving.

May crushed one tablet and stirred it into a cup of coconut water. Carefully, she lifted Phuong's head and poured the medicine into her mouth, a little at a time. Then she waited. Hours passed. The tent fell quiet, save for the whisper of waves and the soft rustling of canvas in the wind. On the second day, Phuong's fever broke.

On the third, she opened her eyes. "Mẹ," she whispered. May leaned in, tears slipping down her cheeks.

"Yes, con. Mẹ is here." "You stayed," Phuong murmured. "I never left." Outside the tent, life in the camp went on. Ships still came. Families still prayed to hear their names. But inside May's tent, something sacred had happened, something no ship or country could offer. A child had lived. A mother had held her ground. And May, once again, believed in miracles.

Chapter **10**

Arrogance on the Way to the French

The day the French ship docked again, a wave of hushed excitement swept through the refugee camp. It didn't take long for the news to spread, like a match to dry brush, the whispers leapt from tent to tent: a new list was posted. Another transport. Another handful of names plucked from limbo and tossed toward what some dared to call a future. Hope, desperation, and dread mingled in the crowd as people rushed toward the pier. Most carried nothing but hope in their fists. Some scanned the list with eyes that had done this far too many times. A few wept, whether from joy or grief, it was getting harder to tell.

May didn't go. She didn't need to. There was no hope for her on that ship. Instead, she sat beneath the frayed edge of her tent's canopy, arms folded, eyes fixed on the harbor path. Because she knew who was on that list, and that name brought no joy. Only a bitter knot deep in her chest. The woman. They had arrived together six months ago, clinging to the rails of the same overcrowded boat. Both had watched the Vietnamese shoreline disappear into fog. Both had held on to whatever they could. But even then, the differences were unmistakable. The woman had come alone, no husband, no children, no visible grief. Just herself, polished and poised in a lavender áo dài (traditional Vietnamese long dress) stitched with gold thread. Somehow, the silk remained spotless, untouched by sea spray, rain, or the human crush on the deck.

While others clutched rag bundles and crying toddlers, she stood tall, detached, untouched. Her food was carefully wrapped and portioned for one. Her face was dry. Her hands never reached out to help. Never opened to receive it. May had tried not to judge. Everyone survived in their own way. But it was hard not to notice how the woman moved, intentionally, as though misfortune were beneath her. In the camp, that air of superiority hardened. She never scrambled for food. Never shouted her name at the list readers. She had quiet channels. Somehow, she always had more soap. More sugar. Her earrings stayed polished. Her sandals never broke. Her back never bent.

She didn't speak to mothers like May. Didn't sit with children. Didn't cry at night. She stayed apart. Silent. Intact. And now, her moment had come. May watched her walk toward the French ship like someone boarding a yacht, not escaping a war. No bundle. No photo. No torn remnant of home. Just a neat leather handbag and that same unbothered expression.

Ahead of her, a young mother struggled to lift a toddler and a bag at once. The woman didn't offer help. She stepped around them without a pause. Someone's blanket caught on the railing. The line halted. The woman gave a long, theatrical sigh and shifted her weight, visibly annoyed. She didn't bend down. She didn't speak. She didn't care. May saw it all from a distance. It confirmed what she had always known: The woman had come alone. And she would leave the same way.

While others stumbled forward in disbelief, families clinging to each other, children crying, elders wiping their eyes, the woman boarded with perfect calm. She didn't turn to wave goodbye. She didn't nod in thanks. She disappeared into the ship, into her next life. May stood several yards back, arms crossed, jaw tight. She didn't shout. She didn't spit. She didn't cry. But as the gangway pulled up and the ship drifted from the dock, she leaned forward just slightly and whispered, almost to herself: "Go on. Go to France. And I hope I never see you again." The woman never looked back. The ship moved slowly, casting long shadows over the bay as the last light of day caught the white flag flapping on its mast. The water gurgled beneath it, as if the sea itself were relieved to see her go.

Only when the vessel was a distant blur did May turn away. Behind her, the camp remained, thick with smoke from dinner fires. Children ran barefoot in the dust. Men crouched by the radio station, listening for news. The same old weight of waiting settled over everything. May's name wasn't on any list. No ship waited for her. But one thing was clear.

She would not follow that woman's path. She had come here with her children, with nothing. And she had chosen to suffer with her people, not above them. Her path would be slower. Harsher. But it would be walked with dignity. And when her time came, she would not walk alone. That truth, quiet and steady in her heart, was enough for now.

Chapter 11

A Distant Shore Snake

The refugee camp was a place of hardship, but even amid the waiting and hunger, life somehow continued. Each day brought the same routines, standing in line for rice or water, listening for names that never came, whispering prayers into the damp wind. But in the late afternoons, when the sun softened and the heat gave way to a salty breeze, the children escaped. They raced barefoot to the shoreline, with empty bellies but full voices. They kicked up sand, splashed through the foamy edges of the ocean, built fortresses from driftwood and shells, and chased one another with laughter that didn't belong in a place like this. Older kids called the beach their "kingdom," crowning each other with seaweed and brandishing driftwood swords. Some dug trenches "to protect the little ones from sea monsters." Every splash was a small rebellion, proof that even children of war could find joy in waves and wet sand.

Phuong loved those hours. She wasn't the fastest or the boldest, but something inside her loosened when she stepped into the water. With Khanh and a group of other girls, she waded knee-deep into the shallows, giggling as the tide licked their ankles. For those brief moments, the sea helped them forget the wires, the dirt, and the waiting. But the ocean held danger, too. It happened in an instant. "Snake! Snake!" The shout cracked through the air like a whip.

Children screamed and scattered. Some stumbled backward. Others froze, pointing at the water. Panic rippled through the group. There, not far from Phuong, a long, slick body slithered beneath the surface, black and yellow stripes gliding like ribbons through the waves.

A sea snake. Venomous. Silent. Lethal. And it was heading straight toward her. Phuong couldn't move. Fear gripped her spine. Her breath caught as the creature sliced through the water, its narrow head steady, eyes unblinking.

She blinked as the current tugged at her legs, then she saw it clearly. Just feet away, the sea curled around a long body moving like oil. It was beautiful in a terrible way. She opened her mouth to scream, but no sound came. Her feet felt as if they were glued to the sand. "Phuong, run!" Khanh shouted from behind. But before she could move, a figure sprinted through the shallows. He came from the edge of camp, tall, lean, and quiet as a shadow. The same man who had helped lift her and Sang onto the rescue ship months ago. She remembered his calm, the way he moved like the sea itself, silent and sure.

He never spoke much. Lived alone near the trees. Watched everything. Said nothing. And he always carried a long black Ka-Bar knife at his side, worn, sharp, and clean. He didn't hesitate. In one fluid motion, he drew the blade, raised it, and threw. The knife flew like a streak of light, straight and true. It struck. The snake thrashed once, then fell still. Blood spiraled through the water before both blade and creature vanished beneath a wave. The man stood at the water's edge, eyes fixed on the sea. Phuong ran to him, trembling. Her voice cracked.

"Anh... I'm sorry... you lost your knife... because of me." He looked down at her, quiet and calm. Then knelt and placed a steady hand on her shoulder. "It's just a knife," he said gently. "You're safe. That's what matters." Behind them, the other children gathered in hushed awe. He was no longer just the silent man by the trees. He was something more, someone who had thrown away his last weapon for a child. Phuong held onto him a moment longer. Then they walked back to camp together. That evening, the children burst into the family tent, breathless. "Mẹ! A sea snake! It came right for Phuong!" Khanh cried, her face flushed.

"It was huge, and it swam straight at her!" "But the man from the boat, he saved her!" another added. "He threw his knife into it!" "He lost it in the water, but he didn't care!" May dropped the blanket she was folding. Her hands trembled as she touched Phuong's face. "Are you okay, con?" "I'm okay, Mẹ," Phuong whispered. "He saved me." Minh, listening from the corner, looked up. "The man with the Ka-Bar? The one who helped us on the boat?" Phuong nodded. Minh stood. "I need to speak with him."

He found the man sitting alone near the tree line, repairing a fishing net in the golden light of dusk. "I just wanted to thank you," Minh said. "That was my sister. She's alive because of you." The man nodded slightly. "She's brave." "You threw your knife," Minh said. "That wasn't just a tool. That was history." The man didn't answer. "I'm Minh," he offered quietly. A pause. Then: "Quang." Minh's heart skipped. "Quang? That was the name of my best friend in the army. We fought together near Saigon. But when we saw we had no chance… we deserted. We chose to save our families." Quang looked at him. His eyes said more than words. "I never saw him again," Minh said. "I never even got to say goodbye."

65

A silence passed between them. Then Minh added, "Come with me. My mother would like to thank you." Back in the tent, May looked up from the fire when they entered. "Is this him?" she asked. Minh nodded. "This is Quang." May stood and stepped forward. "You saved my daughter." "I only did what I had to," Quang said softly. "No," May replied. "You did what most wouldn't." She motioned for him to sit. Then, glancing down with a hint of apology, she said, "I'd offer you tea… but we have nothing. The war took everything from us." The three of them sat in a quiet triangle. For a while, no one spoke. The sound of sleeping children filled the silence, and the canvas walls shifted gently in the breeze.

Then May asked, "Do you have family?" Quang's eyes darkened. "I did," he said. "A wife. A son." He stared at the ground. "I wasn't there when it happened. I was stationed outside the city. When I finally got back, it was too late. I couldn't protect them." His voice was flat, as if the pain had been drained from it long ago. "I carried that knife every day after that," he said. "Not just to protect myself. It reminded me of the life I failed to guard." May placed her hand gently over his. "You didn't fail," she said quietly. "You were failed. All of us were." Minh nodded. "We were just boys, told to fight a war that was already lost."

They sat together long into the night, trading fragments of memory, what they had seen, what they had lost, the guilt that clung to every breath. And as the fire burned low and the tent settled into stillness, something had shifted between them. A trust born not of words, but of wounds. When Quang finally rose to leave, May said softly, "Come back tomorrow. Eat with us." He nodded once. And as he stepped into the dark, for the first time in a long while, he didn't feel like a ghost walking through the world.

Chapter **12**

Life in the Refugee Camp

May sat on the rough wooden floor of their makeshift tent, cradling her infant daughter, Ngoc. The baby whimpered, her tiny mouth searching for milk. May adjusted her torn blouse and guided Ngoc to nurse, though she knew her milk was running thin. She wasn't eating enough to sustain her strength, and the hunger gnawed at her body. Outside, the refugee camp buzzed with noise. Red Cross and Red Crescent volunteers moved through the crowd, distributing rice, canned food, and water, but it was never enough. The camp swelled with new arrivals each day: desperate families who had fled Vietnam, just like her. Some were half-starved, their bodies fragile from weeks at sea. Others bore wounds from pirate attacks. The more people arrived, the less there was to go around.

Minh crouched at the tent's entrance, watching the food line "Má," he whispered, "I can try to find work. Some men go to the village to carry sacks or help the fishermen.

Maybe I can earn a little money." May shook her head. "It's dangerous. Some men don't come back." "But we have no choice," Minh replied, his young face hardened by their struggle. "We have no money left, and Ngoc needs you to eat." May looked down at her baby. Ngoc's eyelids fluttered as she nursed, unaware of the hunger surrounding her. May had spent her last coins the week before, trading them for a handful of fish, a few vegetables, and a small bag of rice. Now, she had nothing.

Her other children sat nearby, silent and tired. Chi was trying to stitch a tear in his shirt with a broken needle she had found. The younger ones sat in the sand, their bare feet caked in dirt, eyes sunken from hunger. The camp was not a safe place, especially for women. At night, May lay awake, listening for danger. There were too many desperate people, and not all were kind. The weak were always at risk, the sick, the elderly, and the women without men to protect them. The stench of unwashed bodies and rotting food clung to the humid air. May heard children coughing in nearby tents, a dry, hacking sound that never stopped. She feared illness more than anything. Medicine was rare, and even when the Red Cross had supplies, they were hard to get. You needed connections, or luck.

A mother in the next tent had lost her baby the week before. May had heard the woman's wails echo through the night, cries that sounded like they tore from bone. No one spoke of it now, but everyone remembered. Minh's voice pulled her from her thoughts. "Má, let me try. Just for a little while." She tightened her grip on Ngoc and sighed. She had fought so hard to get them this far, but the fight wasn't over. Looking at Minh, she nodded. "Be careful, con. Don't go alone." Minh nodded, jaw set with determination, and slipped into the crowd. May watched him go, praying for his safety. She kissed the top of Ngoc's head, inhaling her baby's faint, milky scent. No matter how hard things became, she would find a way to survive. For Ngoc. For all of them.

Minh's journey beyond the camp began early the next morning. Before the sun rose, he joined a small group of young men who had arranged work with local fishermen. They spoke little, everyone understood the risks. That day, their job was to help transport goods from a nearby island back to the coastal markets. Minh lifted sacks of rice, crates of vegetables, and bundles of dried fish onto boats and unloaded them at the docks upon return. The pay was meager, just a few coins or scraps of food, but it was something.

The sea was harsh. The wooden boat rocked in the waves, and the sun scorched their backs. Salt and fish clung to their skin. And always, there was the threat of pirates. Boats disappeared. Some returned stripped and broken. Others never returned at all. As they neared the mainland, Minh spotted another boat, silent, dark, and fast. The fisherman beside him turned pale. Tension twisted in Minh's gut as he gripped the edge of the boat. But the strange vessel veered off before reaching them, vanishing into the horizon. Even so, the moment rattled him.

When they docked and finished unloading, the villagers gave them boiled sweet potatoes and a few coins. Minh tucked the food into a cloth bag and clutched the coins tightly in his fist. It had only been one day, but it felt like a lifetime. That night, Minh lay on the sand floor of their tent, sore and restless. He could still hear the waves and the low drone of the pirate boat. He was safe, but only just. He had done it. For now, that was enough. The next morning, he handed May the food and coins without a word. She didn't ask. Her eyes glistened as she took them.

Thanks to Minh's brave effort, the family had just enough to keep going. And though the work had stiffened his back and roughened his hands, Minh stood taller that night. Later that afternoon, a sudden downpour forced many families under fraying tarps or into their tents. Rainwater trickled into the corners of May's shelter, turning the floor to mud. She placed an old sheet beneath Ngoc to keep her dry. The wind rattled the plastic tarp above them, tugging at the ropes.

Long helped secure the edges, hands trembling with exhaustion. "Má," he whispered, "when will this end?" May couldn't answer. She touched his cheek "Soon, con. We just have to hold on a little longer." As night fell, the camp quieted. The rain turned to drizzle, and the sky flickered with distant lightning. May sat awake for a long time, listening to the breath of each child, each inhale, each exhale. Proof they were still alive. She thought of the sea, their escape, all they had endured. And she made herself a promise: they would leave this place. Somehow, someday, she would get them to a better life. In the dark, with Ngoc pressed to her chest, May began to hum a lullaby from home, soft, broken, and full of hope.

Chapter 13

A Hidden Treasure

Long and Duy had been friends for as long as they could remember. But the hardships of refugee life had welded their bond into something deeper, unshakable. Like all the children in the camp, they had no toys, no books, and no school, only each other. Their world was a strip of sun-scorched beach, where waves whispered against the shore and golden sand shimmered beneath the unforgiving sun. It was both their playground and their escape, the only place where they could still feel like children. Every day, after the morning meal, usually a small bowl of rice and watery soup, the children ran to the water, splashing, swimming, and pretending to be captains, heroes, or warriors from the old stories their parents used to tell. These moments gave them a fleeting taste of normal childhood.

But the children never played pirates. They had heard too many real stories of pirate ships attacking refugee boats, stealing what little people carried, sometimes leaving behind worse. Pirates were not make-believe villains; they were a terrifying truth. So instead, the children played safer games: building shelters from bamboo scraps and torn tarps, pretending to cook with sand and leaves, or acting out journeys where everyone made it safely to shore. Even in play, they longed for safety, not danger. Their imaginations, shaped by real threats, turned toward hope, home, and peace. Today was no different. The sun shimmered on the ocean's surface, too bright to look at for long.

Long dove beneath the waves, holding his breath, letting the weightless silence envelop him. That's when he saw it something dark floating just below the surface. At first, he thought it was seaweed. But as he swam closer, he saw that it was man-made. With a few strong strokes, he reached out and grabbed it. His fingers closed around worn leather, soft, waterlogged, but intact. He burst through the surface, gasping for air, raising his hand to examine the object. A wallet. Duy rushed over, eyes wide with curiosity. "What is it?" he asked, peering at the soaked bundle in Long's hand. Long hesitated, his heart thudding. Even at his age, he knew this was important, too important to talk about in the open. He looked around, making sure no one was watching, then tugged Duy aside.

"We have to take this to Má," Long whispered, barely louder than the waves. Duy nodded, sensing the seriousness in his friend's voice. When they arrived, May was sitting inside, cradling Ngoc while Chi continued working on a tear in her shirt, threading the needle as if she were repairing something sacred. Minh had not yet returned from the village. "Má," Long said, breathless, kneeling in front of her. "I found this." He held out the wallet, still dripping.

May's eyes narrowed as she reached for it. She opened it carefully, her fingers flipping through the soaked bills. Her breath caught. She looked at Long, then Duy "Where did you find this?" Long swallowed. "In the water. It was floating." May's thoughts spun. Who had lost it? Was someone looking for it? Could this bring danger to their doorstep? If the wrong people found out, they might accuse Long of stealing. In a place like this, rumors spread fast, and punishment came faster. She glanced down at her sleeping baby, then at the gaunt faces of her children. For a moment, she let herself imagine what the money could do. Food. Medicine. Maybe a small blanket for the baby. But May had lived long enough to know that sudden gifts often came with hidden costs.

She closed the wallet and held it tight "We say nothing," she said firmly. "Not to anyone." Long and Duy nodded in unison. They understood. In the camp, silence was survival. That night, long after the children had fallen asleep, May sat with the wallet in her lap. She turned the wallet over in her hands, fingers tracing its contours, when she saw it. A name, faintly inscribed on the inside flap. The letters were faded, almost ghost-like, but clear enough to read.

It was a foreign name. Western. American. Utterly out of place among the few meager belongings the refugees carried. A chill crept up her spine. It must have belonged to one of the foreigners, the ones who had shaped so much of their fate. She buried the wallet beneath their bedding. She would wait. If no one came asking in the next few days, maybe, only maybe, she'd quietly trade a few bills for food or medicine. But only if she had no other choice. Until then, silence was protection. Outside the tent, the camp fell into uneasy stillness beneath the stars. Somewhere out at sea, a wallet had floated toward two boys. And somehow, perhaps, it had landed exactly where it needed to be.

Chapter **14**

A Dangerous Secret

May's hands trembled as she tucked the damp wallet beneath a folded, threadbare blanket in the most secluded corner of their cramped tent. The leather felt impossibly heavy, not just with water, but with the terrifying weight of possibility. And danger. The refugee camp, she realized, was no longer a place of temporary shelter. It had become a battlefield for survival. Hunger, desperation, and fear had stripped people down to something feral. Even trusted friends, under unbearable pressure, could become dangerous.

She glanced at Long and Duy, who sat near the tent's entrance, their faces streaked with dust from the long run back from the beach "Not a word," she reminded them, her voice a whisper, firm and final. "To anyone." They nodded solemnly. The low sun cast sharp shadows under their tired eyes, making them look older than they were. Outside, the camp buzzed with tension. People shuffled through long

77

food lines, voices rising with frustration as weary Red Cross volunteers announced that supplies were running low. Others huddled in small groups, whispering, eyes constantly scanning the crowd for answers, or threats. Children wandered barefoot in the dust, ribs showing beneath thin shirts, some crying from hunger, others dazed by exhaustion.

May moved through her routine carefully, trying to appear normal while her senses stayed alert. If someone had lost a wallet like this, they'd be searching for it already. Passing a group of grim-faced men by the food stand, she carried an empty, dented can to fill with rice water. A snippet of conversation floated her way. "I swear it was in my pocket when we left the boat," one said, his voice tight. "Then you dropped it in the sea," another replied. "It's gone. Probably picked up already. Lost to the waves." May kept walking, heart pounding like a drum in her ears. Was it their wallet? Someone else's? A stranger's? She slowed. Her body tensed. Maybe she should speak, offer it back, stop the whispers before they reached her tent. She turned slightly, readying herself.

Then a woman's voice rang out behind her, clear and relieved: "I found it!" Relief surged through May, loosening her clenched shoulders. She exhaled deeply. But even as her fear receded, unease lingered. If someone could falsely claim a wallet so easily, what would happen if people suspected her family had something valuable? She walked back to the tent, her steps cautious, her body tense. Sitting down, she gently bounced baby Ngoc in her arms, finding comfort in the fragile rhythm of her breathing. Ngoc's legs were frighteningly thin, little more than bone.

She needed Minh. He would know what to do. An hour passed. Then another. The sun dropped behind the horizon, the sky streaked in bruised orange and red. The camp quieted, but the tension grew sharper in the dark. Night was when desperation turned to action. Finally, Minh returned, weaving through the thinning crowd. He carried a small bundle: a few handfuls of rice, some dried fish, wilted greens. His face was pale with fatigue, but his eyes stayed sharp, scanning the camp, sensing something was wrong.

May stood as he entered. "Minh," she whispered urgently. "We have a problem." She reached under the blanket and pulled out the wallet. Opening it just enough to show the stack of American bills, she let the green catch the low light. Minh's eyes widened. Then narrowed. "Where did you get this?" he asked, voice low and tense. Long spoke up quickly, his voice shaking. "I found it in the water." Minh let out a slow, heavy breath, rubbing a hand over his face.

"This... this is real money, Má," he murmured, his tone reverent. "This could change everything." May nodded, but the fear in her chest overpowered any spark of hope. "Or it could destroy us." Minh sank beside her, thoughtful. "If someone's looking for this, we have to be careful. If we use it, people will ask questions. If anyone finds out..." He didn't finish. He didn't need to.

May looked at her children, their sunken cheeks, the dullness in their eyes. She imagined what the money could do: medicine for Ngoc, shoes to protect their feet, a small treat to bring joy. But she also saw the risks: an accusation, a rumor, a theft. One careless word could expose them to everyone's hunger. She had learned to fear anything that came too easily. Gifts often carried unseen costs. She turned the wallet in her hands, tracing its stitching. Who had it belonged to? What journey had brought it to her? She gripped it tighter and whispered, fierce and quiet: "We wait. And we watch."

Chapter **15**

Testing the Money

For days, May kept the wallet hidden beneath their bedding, listening carefully to the whispers around the camp. No one seemed to be searching for lost money, and no fights had broken out over a missing wallet. The tension that once clung to her shoulders began to ease, just slightly. Perhaps just perhaps, this was a gift, a hidden chance from fate.

On the third day, after feeding Ngoc and making sure the younger children were occupied, May reached under the blanket and pulled out the wallet. The leather had dried, but salt-stained marks still lined its surface. She flipped through the crisp green bills, her fingers trembling. Each one felt like both salvation and danger.

She turned to Minh, who watched quietly from the corner of the tent. Her voice was barely a whisper. "Take one." She pulled out a five-dollar bill and pressed it into his hand. "Go and try to buy something. Just something small. We need to know if this is real." Minh hesitated, staring at

81

the foreign paper in his palm. He had never held American money before, but he understood its power. If it worked if it was real they had more than food. They had a future.

"What if someone asks where I got it?" he asked. "Tell them you worked for it," May replied quickly. "But be careful. If you sense anything strange, walk away." Minh nodded. He tucked the bill inside his waistband, beneath his shirt, and slipped out of the tent. May watched him disappear into the crowd, her heart thudding. She turned to Long and Duy. "Stay inside," she said. "Don't talk to anyone." They nodded silently. Even at their age, they understood the weight of the moment.

Minh moved quickly through the dusty paths toward the southern edge of the camp, where a row of makeshift stalls had sprung up.

Though the Red Cross and Red Crescent provided rations, an underground market had flourished, barter and trade blooming in desperation. Vendors sat beneath worn tarps stretched over crates, selling everything from canned fish and threadbare shirts to ginger root, dried bananas, and sandals made from old tires. The air smelled of sweat, salt, and something sweet cooking over an open flame. Minh felt every heartbeat like a hammer in his chest. The five-dollar bill burned against his skin. Each glance from a passerby made his palms sweat. He kept his head down and moved fast.

At last, he stopped at an older woman's stall. Bundles of rice and strips of dried mango were arranged in neat rows. Her gray hair was tied back in a tight bun, and her sun-darkened face was deeply lined. A faded floral scarf draped her shoulders. Her hands were knotted but sure, and her eyes sharp, intelligent watched him closely. Minh cleared his throat. "How much for a handful of rice?" "Two Malaysian ringgit," she replied, without looking up. Minh hesitated, then pulled the folded U.S. bill from his waistband. "Do you take this?" Her eyes widened, just slightly. She looked up and scanned the area around them. Her expression tightened.

"American money?" she asked, voice low. "Where'd you get it?" "I worked for a man near the village," Minh said. His voice cracked slightly. His mouth had gone dry. She took the bill slowly and examined it with practiced care. She rubbed it between her fingers, held it to the light, bent it at the corners. The silence stretched on. Minh's stomach knotted tighter with each passing second. Finally, she nodded. "American money is good," she said quietly. "But be careful who you show it to." She reached into a rusted tin box and pulled out a few wrinkled one-dollar bills and a handful of Malaysian coins. Then, without a word, she handed him a modest bag of rice. Minh let out a breath he hadn't realized he was holding. His legs felt weak. He thanked her quickly, slipped the change into his pocket, and walked briskly back toward the tent, never once looking back.

When Minh returned, May spotted him from across the clearing. She rose quickly and met him halfway, her face pale with anticipation. "Well?" she whispered, her voice trembling. Minh held up the bag of rice and a small handful of change. "It worked," he said quietly. "It's real." May stared at the rice, then at the money. For a moment, hope flared in her chest like a match struck in darkness. Back in the tent, she sat beside Minh as he recounted every detail of the exchange. The woman's warning echoed in her mind: Be careful who you show it to. She looked down at the remaining stack of bills inside the wallet. They were no longer just paper. They carried power. And in a place like this, power could be dangerous.

"We must go slow," she said at last. "Very slow. We can't draw attention. A little at a time." Minh nodded. Across the tent, Long and Duy sat silently, their wide eyes fixed on their mother and brother. The air felt heavier now, charged with the weight of new knowledge, equal parts thrilling and terrifying. In the distance, a baby cried. Someone laughed.

But inside their small patch of the camp, everything had changed. The money was real. And so was the danger. They had passed the first test. Now came the harder one, using it without losing everything.

Chapter 16

The Arrival

As the months passed, the camp grew crowded with new faces and fresh stories, while familiar ones quietly disappeared. Every few weeks, a ship arrived in the harbor, carrying away groups of refugees to distant shores. With each departure, the crowd May had once arrived with thinned, friends, neighbors, and strangers vanishing beyond the sea, leaving behind only those still waiting, suspended in limbo. Some were bound for France. Others for Australia, Japan, or Canada. Families wept with joy when their names were called. Hope lit their eyes as they boarded, their tears a mixture of relief and sorrow. The once tight-knit community fractured with every departing vessel.

But May remained. She stayed because she believed, no, she knew, the Americans would come. They had to. She refused to beg another nation. The war had already taken everything from her: her husband, her home, her dignity. Now, the country that helped cause that war owed her something, not for herself, but for her children. Life at the camp followed a steady rhythm. Morning prayers whispered into the rising sun. Long waits in food lines. Children playing by the shore. Adults exchanging quiet conversations and cautious hopes. The camp felt like a place holding its breath, waiting to empty. But it only grew more crowded. Then one morning, the air shifted.

A wave of sound surged through the camp, shouts, laughter, running footsteps. May rushed outside, heart pounding, just in time to see it: a ship cutting through the bay like a promise. An enormous American flag billowed from the mast, catching the morning light. She froze. Tears welled in her eyes. Her voice trembled. "Minh! It's them. Get your brothers and sisters. Now." Minh didn't ask. He ran. By the time he returned, breathless and tugging Hoang and the younger children behind him, the ship had docked. Uniformed American officers had set up barricades and formed a line. Names were called from clipboards. Families with matching entries were let through. Others were turned away, gently, but firmly.

May stood in line, gripping her children's hands so tightly her knuckles turned white. When they reached the front, a young officer flanked by a Vietnamese translator looked up. "Name?" May straightened her back. "May Ninh

Chau." The translator repeated it. The officer scanned his clipboard, once, twice, then shook his head. "I'm sorry. You're not on the list. Please step aside." "No," May said firmly. "I waited. I believed you would come. You must take us." "Ma'am," the officer said calmly, "you're holding up the line." "You brought us to this," she snapped. "You must solve it." "Ma'am, I understand you're upset, but I need you to remain calm so we can, "

"Calm?" May's voice rose. "You want me to be calm while you decide my children's future like it means nothing? I won't let you decide for them!" The officer raised a hand. "Watch your tone, ma'am." "No, you watch what you're doing. If you think I'll stand here quietly and accept this, you picked the wrong mother." Beside her, little Sang clung to her shirt. "Mama... what's happening?" May knelt and kissed her daughter's forehead. "Không sao đâu con, mẹ ở đây." It's okay, baby. I'm here. She stood again, trembling. The air buzzed with tension. Then a ripple of murmurs passed through the line. A man in a white naval uniform stepped forward from the deck, the captain. He had been watching. He saw the fire in May's eyes, the pain behind her defiance, and the child weeping at her side.

With a short nod, he spoke to two officers. They approached gently. "Ma'am," one said, voice softer now, "please come with us. The captain would like to speak with you." May hesitated, her eyes darting. "It's okay," the officer added. "He wants to help." They led her up the ramp. Her children followed closely, Sang still clinging to her side. The captain stood tall on the deck, weathered and sunburned. His eyes met May's, not seeing a refugee, but a mother who had fought for every breath, every step. He stepped forward and extended his hand. "Mama, I would be happy to bring you to America." May didn't understand the words. But she understood his face, the warmth in his voice, the way his hand reached not just to her, but to her children.

He gestured toward the ship. "Welcome aboard." Tears streamed down her face. "Cảm ơn... cảm ơn ông trời..." she whispered. Thank you. Thank you, Heaven. The captain knelt beside Sang, brushing a tear from her cheek. "You don't have to cry," he said softly. "We're going to take you home." Sang stopped crying, not because she understood, but because her mother was smiling again. And for now, that was enough.

Chapter 17

The Long Journey

The ship groaned as it pulled away from the harbor, carrying May and her children out of the refugee camp and into the unknown. The shoreline of Southeast Asia faded behind them, swallowed by mist and distance. This was a passenger ship, nothing like the small, overloaded boats that had once carried them to safety. This one was built for distance. It had towering decks, echoing halls, and the thick smell of oil and salt that clung to every surface. The hum of the engine vibrated beneath their feet like a steady heartbeat. On the main deck, families huddled beneath wool blankets. Some were assigned cabins, tiny compartments with metal bunks, barely big enough for a mother and child to lie down.

Others claimed space in corridors or corners, wherever they could. May and her children were among the lucky ones. Their small cabin wasn't much, but it had a door they could lose, a place to rest without constant fear. May sat with her back against a crate, arms wrapped tightly around

Sang, Duy, and Long. Minh stood nearby, leaning against the wall, his gaze fixed on the rolling waves. Hoang sat cross-legged on the floor, sketching with a dull pencil on a scrap of paper, a makeshift journal of the life they'd left behind. The first night at sea was rough. The ship pitched violently in the waves. Children vomited over the rails. Mothers rocked their babies until their arms ached. Many grew seasick, their faces pale and clammy. Buckets lined the hallways. Cans clattered across the galley floor. But no one complained. To be on this ship at all was a miracle.

Each day followed a rhythm. Three times a day, crew members handed out meals in plastic containers: steamed rice, a hard-boiled egg, a slice of Spam, and watery vegetable broth. It was more food than they'd seen in months, and none went to waste. The American crew moved quietly, often with downcast eyes. They offered help where they could, an extra blanket, a kind word. Language was a barrier, but gestures and smiles often bridged the gap. At night, the common areas filled with murmured conversation. Few people slept. Many sat in circles, whispering dreams. Parents spoke the names of loved ones left behind. Children clung to their mothers, wide-eyed and uncertain.

Joy flickered in small bursts, a quiet laugh, a lullaby hummed in the dark, a shared memory that softened even the hardest faces. But every emotion passed through a filter of exhaustion and guarded hope. They were still in limbo, not yet free, not yet safe. One evening, as golden light spilled over the deck, Sang tugged May's sleeve. "Mama… are we in America yet?" May smiled and brushed a lock of hair from her daughter's face. "Not yet, con yêu. But we're closer than we've ever been." That night, May lay awake, staring at the metal ceiling of their cabin. She listened to the soft breathing of her children and whispered a prayer, not for herself, but for the strength to endure. Strength to keep going. Strength to protect them. Strength to be enough.

Then, after many days at sea, a new silhouette emerged on the horizon, lush green trees, tropical flowers, and low buildings ringed with fencing and guards. They had arrived in Guam. As the ship pulled into port, a hush fell over the passengers. This was not their final destination, but it was a step in the right direction. A real, tangible step. Soldiers stood in neat rows along the dock. As the ramp lowered, they moved quickly, lifting elderly refugees from their seats, carrying sleeping toddlers, offering hands to help others down. Medical personnel waited at the arrival zone. Clad in white and khaki uniforms, they checked temperatures, asked questions through interpreters, and handed out hygiene kits. May stood still as one nurse gently examined Sang and

Long, then waved them through. May was overwhelmed. The order. The care. The quiet efficiency of it all. It was unlike anything she had known since the war began. There was no shouting. No pushing. No chaos. Only calm, steady help. Nearby, American volunteers handed out juice boxes and snacks. When Sang received one, along with a pack of cookies, her eyes lit up in disbelief.

She looked at May with wonder. "Is this for me?" she asked, holding the unopened box. May nodded, her throat tight. A young woman in a Red Cross vest stepped forward and smiled. "Welcome," she said gently, her voice filled with sincerity. May almost cried. She had spent years surviving, fighting for scraps, shielding her children, watching good people fall through the cracks. Now someone was offering them juice. And kindness. She took Sang's hand and whispered, "We made it. We're here." And for the first time in a long time, May allowed herself to believe: Maybe things will get better.

Chapter **18**

Arriving at Guam Island

It was the first time in years that May saw buildings that didn't look broken, or people who didn't look afraid. It wasn't the America she had imagined, but everything here was strange in a peaceful way. There were rows of clean tents, running water, and smiling strangers. The air smelled faintly of sea salt and soap, clean, soft, unfamiliar. For the first time in ages, they were surrounded by order. American nurses in white uniforms handed out toothbrushes, combs, and fresh clothes folded into brown paper bags. May watched, eyes wide, as each of her children received something of their own, socks, shirts, even underwear. Such small items felt like treasures. There were lines for medical checks, lines for food, and volunteers handing out toys and coloring books. Duy and Long stared, wide-eyed, at a water fountain.

"Can we drink from the wall?" Long whispered.

"Yes," May said, watching their wonder. "It's clean." They

had never seen so much fresh water freely given. Duy pressed the button cautiously, and when the stream burst forth, he jumped back and giggled. Minh, always curious, tried a slice of pizza from one of the food tents. He chewed slowly, then made a face. "It tastes like ketchup and cheese on bánh mì." Hoang laughed, already heading back for seconds. "I like it," he said. "It's strange... but good."

Children with juice boxes and crackers skipped past them. May sat beneath the shade of a large tent canopy, Sang curled in her lap. A nurse handed her a packet with bandages, ointment, and vitamins. Another passed her a small bottle of shampoo. "Thank you," May whispered. She wasn't sure if they understood, but she was grateful nonetheless. The children received not just food, but warmth. A volunteer handed Sang a soft pink blanket, and she clutched it to her chest like a prize. Long received a rubber ball. Duy, a deck of animal cards.

Then a volunteer with bright eyes and a clipboard approached their tent. "May Ninh Chau?" May stood "Yes?" The woman smiled. "You and your family are being transferred." May's heart leapt. "To where?" The woman checked her list. "Idaho." May repeated it, uncertain. "Ai-đa-hô?" "Yes," the woman nodded. "It's cold. But it's safe.

And a sponsor is waiting." May nodded slowly, absorbing the words: cold, safe, sponsor.

That evening, while her children played nearby, May sat beside another mother from a different tent. The woman spoke softly of her daughter, who still woke screaming at night, terrified by the closed room. "They said it's called... stress," she said, searching for the word. "The doctors here... they call it trauma. They're trying to help." May listened silently. Her own children had survived so much, days adrift at sea, hunger, the snake, the storm, but they still smiled. Still laughed. Were they stronger? Or were their wounds just hidden deeper? Later that night, after lights dimmed and the children slept, May lay on her thin cot, drifting in and out of uneasy dreams. From the next tent over came a sharp, shattering sound: a child's voice, loud and panicked, sobbing and gasping for breath. It wasn't the cry of hunger or exhaustion, it was deeper, primal, full of terror.

She heard a woman's voice trying to soothe the child, but the sobs only grew louder, ragged, wild. Then the woman began crying too, her voice breaking under the weight of her grief. A nurse arrived, calm and practiced. Footsteps shuffled. Water was offered. Gentle reassurances followed. May sat up slowly, clutching her chest. Her hand reached instinctively for Sang, who stirred but did not wake. That's when it truly hit her, her children were safe. Not untouched, but sleeping peacefully. She pressed her forehead to her knees. "Cảm ơn trời... cảm ơn..." Thank you, Heaven. Thank you.

She had no name for what she'd heard that night, but she knew what it meant: the war still lived inside some of them, even if the bombs had stopped falling. Some children had left the battlefield, but the battlefield had not left them. The next morning, May overheard two nurses talking. "So many kids with nightmares," one said. "Flashbacks. Panic. We're trying to screen for PTSD. Some of the adults, too. They've seen too much." May didn't know what PTSD meant, but she understood suffering. And suddenly, she felt something unexpected, not just grief, not guilt, but luck. Her children were still whole. Not untouched, but somehow... still light inside.

Chapter 19

From Guam to USA

After two long weeks at the refugee processing center in Guam, May and her children were finally cleared for travel. It was early October 1975, and the tropical air still clung to their clothes as they boarded a massive Boeing 707 jetliner, May's first time on a plane. She clutched their worn duffel bag tightly, the hum of engines vibrating under her feet, as they shuffled down the aisle. Sang's small hand was damp in hers.

The cabin, even in economy, felt vast compared to anything she'd known. Rows of seats stretched forward and back, the air conditioning a crisp, unfamiliar chill against her skin. As they buckled in, the plane began to taxi, the engines growing louder, a low, steady roar building beneath them. When the wheels finally left the earth and the nose tilted upward, Sang's eyes went wide with alarm.

"Mama!" she cried, her voice trembling. "Are we falling?!"

May wrapped an arm around her, pulling her close as the pressure pushed them back into their seats. "No, baby," she whispered, her own heart pounding. "We're flying. Just like the birds."

Sang pressed her face to the window. Below, the patchwork of streets and houses gave way to endless clouds, soft and white, stretching beneath them like fields of cotton. May watched too, the unfamiliar sight stirring something quiet inside her. For the first time in years, the world below felt distant, the past left behind, shrinking with every mile. For the first time, she thought: We're going somewhere. Not running. Not hiding. Moving forward.

A Stop In Okinawa

Hours later, as the sun dipped toward the horizon, a soft chime sounded. The captain's voice crackled over the intercom:

"Ladies and gentlemen, we'll soon be landing at Naha Airport in Okinawa, Japan, for a scheduled refueling stop. We anticipate being on the ground for approximately one hour and fifteen minutes. Passengers are requested to deplane and proceed to the transit lounge."

A moment later, a calm, clear voice repeated the instructions in rapid, flowing Vietnamese. In the strangeness of their journey, hearing her native tongue was a small, comforting anchor for May.

She felt a flutter in her stomach, nervous, uncertain. Another stop. She had hoped for a straight path, but nothing was truly straight in this new life. As the Boeing 707 taxied to a halt and the engines sighed into silence, passengers unbuckled and murmured, reaching for bags and children. Sang, now groggy, clung to May as they stepped into the jetway.

The terminal felt like another world. The air was cooler and drier than Guam's heavy humidity, and a faint scent of jet fuel lingered. Inside, the transit lounge was bright and orderly, with polished floors and vending machines lined with colorful snacks. Airport staff moved with quiet precision. Sang's alarm gave way to wonder. She marveled at the machines and the tiny cans of juice behind glass, the way everything clicked and whirred.

May led them to a quiet corner where she nursed baby Ngoc and changed her diaper on a soft cloth she'd carried from Saigon. Minh and Chi, older but no less nervous, stood nearby watching the others, holding tight to each other.

Out the wide windows, May watched a silent choreography unfold on the tarmac. Brightly vested ground crew guided massive tanker trucks into position beneath the wings. Thick hoses snaked from trucks to plane, fueling it with the precision of surgery. May noticed one worker tapping gauges, another speaking into a headset, both part of a carefully timed ritual. Every movement purposeful.

The seventy-five minutes passed both quickly and slowly. Around them, passengers stretched, sipped hot tea from paper cups, used the gleaming restrooms, or simply sat in silence. May held Sang close again, the child's head resting on her chest, and stared through the glass.

Then, a final boarding call rang out, first in English, then in Vietnamese. They gathered their things and reboarded, returning to the same seats, now familiar. The plane felt heavier, not just with fuel but with everything it carried: people, grief, and quiet hope.

As the doors sealed and the engines stirred back to life, May glanced out once more at the orderly lights of Okinawa. It had been a clean pause, a breath between storms. And now they were moving forward again. America was still far away, but closer than it had ever been.

The Long Stretch to Honolulu

May watched the Japanese coastline dissolve beneath the clouds, a fleeting image in a world that seemed to shift with each passing hour. The captain's voice broke through the hum of the engines, announcing their next leg: several more hours eastward to Honolulu, Hawaii, where they would make a brief stop before the final push to the mainland.

The reality of the journey had begun to weigh heavily. The novelty of flight, once thrilling, had long since faded, replaced by a bone-deep weariness. Around her, passengers dozed in varying states of discomfort, heads tilted against small plastic pillows. Lucky them, May thought with a pang of envy. Sleep remained elusive. She closed her eyes and focused on the rhythmic churn of the engines, hoping to coax her mind into stillness. But the quiet unearthed old memories. Faces blurred by time. Voices she might never hear again.

Her thoughts always returned to the children. Sang, usually full of chatter, was now pale and quiet, her body curled against May's side. Minh and Chi sat upright, eyes darting across the unfamiliar cabin, trying to be brave. Baby

Ngoc, mercifully, slept on from her earlier feeding in Okinawa, but May knew the peace wouldn't last.

Time passed in slow motion. Her legs throbbed from sitting so long. She shifted often, trying to stretch without disturbing the children. The air inside the plane, though cool, was dry and stale. Her lips cracked. Her back ached. Still, she did not complain. This was the price of reaching a new world.

Finally, after what felt like an eternity suspended between sky and sea, she sensed descent. May leaned toward the window. The Hawaiian Islands appeared, lush, green peaks rising from the blue, rimmed by ribbons of turquoise surf. A postcard scene. A paradise. But May's heart, too full of fatigue and fear, could barely register the beauty.

The Boeing landed smoothly at Honolulu International Airport. As the plane taxied, a gentle murmur spread through the cabin. Passengers stirred. Seatbelts clicked open. Bags shuffled down from overhead bins. When the doors opened, a wave of warm, fragrant air swept inside, carrying the scent of plumeria blossoms and sea salt. A smell so familiar it almost broke her.

Disembarking, May held sleepy Ngoc close while Sang clung to her skirt, her small face drawn and pale. Minh and Chi followed quietly, eyes scanning the terminal with a mix of wonder and wariness. The atmosphere in Honolulu buzzed with a kind of casual ease, sunhats, surfboards, English spoken with laughter and leisure. But for May, there was no ease. No vacation. Only the ache of muscles and the press of uncertainty.

She scanned the crowd, absorbing the brightness of the lights, the blur of unfamiliar faces. This was another stop. Another place they would not stay. She adjusted Ngoc in her arms, tightened her grip on Sang's hand, and moved forward, step by aching step. Her only compass: the distant promise of California.

The final flight awaited. And with it, whatever would come next.

Chapter **20**

Arriving at Camp Pendleton, California

Just when it felt like the journey would never end when the air inside the plane had gone dry and stale, when May's muscles ached from cradling Ngoc, and the children had fallen in and out of uneasy sleep more times than she could count, the intercom crackled to life. A soft ding, then a voice, a thread of light in the dim cabin:

"Ladies and gentlemen, this is your captain speaking. We'll be landing shortly at Marine Corps Air Station El Toro. Welcome to the United States of America."

Gasps rippled through the cabin. Movements paused midair. A stunned hush followed, broken only by the quiet weeping of a woman near the back. May pressed a hand to her chest. She didn't understand every word, but landing… America, those were enough. Her breath caught. Her heart swelled with cautious joy. Could it be real?

She turned to Minh. His eyes sparkled, but he said nothing. There were no words left. Not now.

The wheels touched down with a long, groaning screech. For a moment, everyone held their breath. Then, as the aircraft slowed, someone whispered, "We're here."

The doors hissed open, and a flood of white light poured into the cabin. Outside, the tarmac of El Toro glowed under harsh floodlights. The massive plane sat still beneath a halo of beams, its wings casting long shadows across warm concrete.

May stepped out into the night, Ngoc clinging to her hip. The air smelled of rubber, diesel, and scorched pavement, strange and sterile, yet safer than anything she'd breathed in months. This was America.

Soldiers stood at intervals, guiding them forward with calm gestures and quiet voices. May didn't understand their English, but their tone was kind, their faces patient. That was enough.

She followed the others toward a line of olive-green military buses. Their engines rumbled steadily, waiting. Sang clung to Minh's hand. Chi looked behind them once, counting their siblings. Around them, families moved like shadows, slow, quiet, wide-eyed. A boy just older than Minh carried his baby sister wrapped in a thin towel. An old man leaned on a young woman's arm. Everyone was exhausted, but no one complained.

At the bus steps, a Marine helped May lift Ngoc, then steadied her as she climbed aboard. The interior smelled faintly of canvas and dust. The seats were worn but padded, cleaner than anything they'd sat on in the camps.

They took seats near the middle. Minh slid into the window, wiping the fog with his sleeve. May sat in the aisle, pulling Sang and Ngoc close. Chi settled behind them next to a quiet boy his age, who stared blankly out the window.

The engine groaned, and the bus jerked into motion. They rolled away from the glowing lights of El Toro into the waiting dark. The base gave way to empty roads and low hills under a moonless sky.

Inside, silence fell. Most passengers were too tired to speak. Mothers cradled sleeping children, their heads resting on shoulders or wrapped in donated jackets. A few whispered prayers in Vietnamese. Near the back, an old woman clutched her rosary, lips moving silently as beads passed through her fingers. A baby whimpered once, but the mother gently hushed it, rocking in rhythm with the road.

May said nothing. She watched the black highway roll by like a river of shadows. She didn't know where they were going, only that someone had said Camp Pendleton. She imagined it as a place with walls. With food. With beds. With answers.

Nearly an hour later, faint lights appeared ahead. A wide gate emerged between tall fencing and sand-colored buildings. Armed guards stood under a checkpoint hut bathed in floodlight. The bus slowed. A soldier stepped out, spoke with the gate team. Flashlights swept gently along the windows, then dipped in quiet acknowledgment.

The gate creaked open. The bus rolled forward into the vast base.

Inside, heads began to rise. Children rubbed their eyes. Even the adults straightened slightly. The grounds were quiet and open, stretching into darkness. Then, ahead: floodlights illuminating rows of white military tents. A hand-painted sign on a wooden post read simply: Refugee Reception Area.

The bus turned onto a gravel road and came to a stop. More buses were already parked nearby, engines humming low. Soldiers moved between them, organizing the arrivals.

The door opened with a groan. A tall Marine stepped in and lifted a hand.

"Welcome to Camp Pendleton."

May didn't understand the words. But she didn't need to. She felt them.

Minh helped Sang down the aisle. Chi followed. May carried Ngoc, now fast asleep again. The night air was cool and sharp against their skin. The sky above them was deep and vast spilled over with stars.

The vast base pulsed with quiet but constant activity, bathed in the harsh, purposeful glow of floodlights that pierced the darkness. Powerful beams illuminated endless rows of canvas tents and low-slung wooden barracks, arranged with near-military precision.

Volunteers in bright Red Cross vests moved through the night with calm efficiency and genuine kindness, gently guiding the steady stream of weary families toward their temporary housing. May instinctively clutched her children closer, their small, warm bodies grounding her, as they were assigned to a bunkhouse. This shared space, home for now to three other families, would become a brief haven for the displaced. Each occupant carried the same burdens: loss, escape, and the profound uncertainty of exile.

They spent four more days at Camp Pendleton, a liminal space suspended between their fractured past and a still-unwritten future. During this time, compassionate Vietnamese translators worked tirelessly to bridge the language barrier for May, their voices soft but steady as they conveyed essential information. Caseworkers, gentle but direct, posed the question that felt both simple and immense: "Where would you like to go?"

May, her strength forged through endurance, answered with quiet certainty. "Anywhere. Just not back."

As if by a quiet miracle, a Lutheran church group from distant Idaho had volunteered to sponsor a refugee family. A kind-hearted farmer named Mr. John saw May's name on a long list and offered, without hesitation, to take in her entire family. His act of generosity felt like a lifeline tossed across oceans.

By the end of the week, a blur of forms, instructions, and quiet, unspoken fears, they were once again boarding a commercial flight. This time, the resettlement agency had arranged for their journey from San Diego to Boise, Idaho.

The children, now more familiar with flying but still wide-eyed, had never been on a plane quite like this. The seats felt soft and padded, a welcome change from the hard benches of previous travels. Glossy magazines peeked from the seat pockets, filled with colorful images of a world still foreign and dazzling.

A flight attendant with a warm smile moved down the aisle, offering small cups of sweet orange juice and bubbly Coca-Cola. The children accepted them with awe, simple luxuries that brought tentative smiles and flickers of wonder. Long, ever the watchful older brother, held Duy's hand tightly the entire flight, a silent promise of safety and protection as they crossed into the unknown.

Chapter 21

Arriving at Boise, Idaho

When the airport doors in Boise, Idaho, finally slid open with a soft, whooshing hiss, a sharp gust of cold, crisp air swept through the terminal and enveloped them. For the first time in their lives, the children watched in awe as their breath curled into tiny clouds before their faces, a visible sign of the chill. May turned slowly, her eyes wide with a blend of apprehension and quiet awe, trying to absorb every detail of this strange, foreign place.

There were no palm trees swaying in humid air. No vast, blue ocean stretching to the horizon. No thick, tropical heat clung to their skin. Instead, there was a vast, endless sky above and sprawling brown fields rolling into a hazy, unfamiliar distance, an entirely different kind of beauty.

Waiting near the entrance, a beacon of hope amid this stark new landscape, stood Mrs. Meier. She held a simple cardboard sign with hand-drawn lettering: "Welcome May's

Family." When her eyes met the tired, uncertain group descending the escalator, she stepped forward without hesitation. She embraced May in a gentle but firm hug, a gesture of warmth and acceptance that needed no translation.

Her voice, soft but steady, carried more than words "Welcome. You're safe now." May didn't understand the exact English, but the meaning reached her heart. The embrace, the tone, the kindness, it all radiated a sense of safety. The warmth from Mrs. Meier's arms was a stark contrast to the cold air outside.

May looked up at the vast gray sky, then down at the snow crunching softly underfoot, its texture completely foreign. She instinctively pulled her children closer, gathering them into her protective embrace.

This is not where we came from, she thought, but maybe... this is where we begin again.

They were driven to a small, modest apartment in a town just outside Boise. The church group had prepared the space with quiet care: warm clothing, canned food, and even a few simple toys for the children. It was a humble but heartfelt welcome.

That night, exhausted beyond words after their long, life-changing journey across continents and cultures, the family collapsed into sleep. For the first time in what felt like forever, they lay on soft beds, their bodies sinking into true rest. All except May.

She stood at the window, the only one awake, gazing out at the snowy stillness beyond the glass. Everything looked so different from the world she'd left behind, so silent, so cold, so still. She pressed her fingers gently to the glass and whispered into the night: We made it.

The next morning, Mrs. Meier arrived promptly, her smile now familiar and deeply comforting. She came to take them on the final leg of their journey, from Boise to the neighboring town of Nampa.

The children pressed their faces to the cold windows of the car, wide-eyed, watching fields of pale, yellowed grass and scattered homes pass beneath the gray October sky.

May sat upright in the front seat, baby Ngoc cradled in one arm, Trong's small hand held tightly in the other. Her heart brimmed with a complicated mixture: deep gratitude, persistent fear of the unknown, and the kind of exhaustion that ran deeper than sleep.

Each passing mile brought them closer to the life they had dared to hope for, yet not fully dared to trust.

They pulled into a quiet apartment complex, two-story buildings with beige siding facing a tidy green courtyard. Their new home was on the second floor: three small bedrooms, a narrow hallway, and a kitchen with avocado-green cabinets, a distinctly American color that struck May as peculiar, but cheerful. It wasn't grand. It wasn't home yet. But it was a beginning.

A New Beginning

May's family stood together at the threshold of their new home, taking in their new surroundings. Everything felt strange, but there was also something else: hope.

For the first time in a long while, they were no longer living in tents, no longer surrounded by the chaos of the refugee camp. Instead, they were in a real apartment. A home. There was a bed for everyone, a space where they could lay their heads without the fear of what the next day might bring. It was a simple home, modest, but it was theirs.

May walked through the rooms slowly, taking it all in, the warmth of the heater, the quiet hum of the refrigerator. It was all so different from the refugee camp, where they had lived with only the bare essentials, struggling to make ends meet. Here, they had things they had once only dreamed of: privacy, a roof over their heads, the comfort of walls and floors that didn't shift beneath them.

Volunteer groups from the community had been quick to offer their help. They brought clothes, blankets, and kitchen supplies. The local church members had organized food drives, gathering everything from canned goods to fresh vegetables, ensuring the family had what they needed to survive the cold winter months.

For May, each small gesture of kindness felt like a piece of the puzzle coming together. She had come to this land with nothing but her determination, but now, she could see the pieces of a new life falling into place.

She glanced around the apartment again, feeling a deep sense of gratitude. It was hard to imagine that just a few months ago, she had been standing in the refugee camp, waiting for a ship to take them to America. And now, here they were. Everything was finally moving in the right direction.

Gradually, life folded into a steadier rhythm, one shaped by quiet resolve and newfound purpose. The chaos of survival gave way to routine: the predictable hum of morning alarms, the careful planning of each day, the soft rituals that marked progress in this strange but hopeful land.

With every sunrise, they built something stronger, small victories layered like bricks in a foundation they never thought they'd have again.

The church, a steadfast pillar of support, soon started English classes, a vital lifeline for new arrivals. Held twice a week in a small, utilitarian room near the main church building, the sessions were led by volunteers: retired teachers, eager college students, and kind strangers from the community. They sat patiently with the refugees, using flashcards, colorful storybooks, and even children's games to teach the basics of the English language.

"Hello." "My name is May." "How are you?" "Thank you very much."

May practiced these phrases every single day. Her accent was thick, a melodic trace of her homeland clinging to each syllable, but her determination was thicker still. She copied each word and phrase meticulously into a small, spiral-bound notebook, a cherished tool in her journey. At dinner, she quizzed her children, turning lessons into shared family games. Sometimes, the kids, quick to pick up the new sounds, would laugh at her pronunciation. May laughed too. Then, with a teasing but firm gleam in her eye, she'd make them repeat the word three times perfectly. They all learned together.

The church also helped in more practical ways, bridging the gap between their past and the uncertain American present.

They found Minh a part-time job washing dishes at a busy local diner, his first paid work in America. For Hoang, they arranged after-school tutoring, recognizing his hunger to learn. And Mrs. Lewis, a gentle woman with practical wisdom, arrived one afternoon carrying a stack of sewing patterns. She patiently taught May how to use a sewing machine.

"You can make clothes or fix them for your family," she said kindly. "Or maybe even sell them, if you get good enough."

It was a simple suggestion, but to May, it sparked something deeper, a glimmer of self-reliance.

Second Sunday in America

The sky was still an inky blue-black when May woke, the world outside cloaked in the silence of a predawn autumn morning. The apartment was cold. The old heater clanked softly in the corner, groaning like an exhausted old man trying his best to wake. May slipped out from under the covers, the floor shocking against her bare feet, and gently roused each child. "Dậy đi các con," she whispered. Wake up, children. Then softly added, "It's time for church."

Minh groaned under the blankets. "It's Sunday, Má... It's 5 a.m. and still dark." May smiled in the dim light. "That's why we go," she replied quietly, her voice layered with meaning, gratitude, purpose, and a quiet defiance of everything they had survived.

They bundled into thick, unfamiliar coats, most of which were too big or too small, but warm, and pulled on clumsy gloves. Then they stepped out into the quiet, frozen street. May didn't know the route perfectly, only what Mrs. Meier had shown her once, from the warmth of her van. But she had memorized each turn like a prayer.

They walked in a line, as they had so many times before. May led, and the children followed behind like ducklings, trudging through knee-deep snow piled along the roadside. Cars passed, their windows fogged with heat. Drivers stared, curious but silent. No one stopped. No one honked, just the occasional glance, detached and fleeting.

The first time May had visited the church, she thought it was close by. Mrs. Meier's van had made the trip seem easy. But walking five miles on foot, every step aching, told a different story. By the time they reached the church, their faces were flushed from cold and effort. Steam rose from their coats like breath.

119

The doors were already open, warm light spilling onto the snowy steps. Inside, heads turned. A mother, followed by nine of her own children and one adopted child from a neighbor, paused at the entrance. The little flock bore the marks of their long walk, their hands aching from the cold and their cheeks raw and flushed by the biting wind. Yet beneath the weariness flickered a quiet pride, mingled with a breath of expectant unease. The children pressed close to their mother, drawn to her warmth and steadiness, encircling her like a living wreath of hope. From a pew near the doorway, Mrs. Meier watched them with a tender smile. Her gentle wave carried more than courtesy; it was a silent vow of comfort, of belonging, of welcome. The pastor paused the service.

"This is May and her family," he announced. "They've come a long, long way to be here today."

May didn't understand the exact words. But she felt the warmth, real, unguarded, in the way people looked at her. She bowed her head and whispered, just loud enough for her children to hear:"Cảm ơn Chúa." Thank God.

Chapter **22**

The Price of a New Life

Minh's hands were raw, chafed, and reddened from hours spent submerged in scalding, soapy water, scrubbing endless piles of greasy dishes. The pungent, sickly-sweet smell of stale cooking grease and leftover food clung persistently to his clothes, seeping into the fabric and his hair, a constant reminder of his work. Yet, he didn't mind it; in fact, he barely noticed. He had a job, a steady, albeit meager, source of income. In this bewildering new country, where every dollar seemed to weigh a thousand pounds, that meant everything. It meant survival, hope, and a tangible contribution to his family's precarious new life.

The restaurant owner, Mr. Blumboum, was a formidable figure. A large man, his expansive belly perpetually stretched the buttons of his white, often grease-stained, button-up shirt to their limit. He had been in the cutthroat restaurant business for decades, his eyes sharp and his mind quick, knowing instinctively how to make the most

121

out of every situation and person who crossed his path. When Minh, barely sixteen and speaking only a smattering of broken English, showed up at the back door of the diner, shoulders hunched with desperation, Blumboum didn't see a struggling refugee. He saw an opportunity, cheap, reliable labor.

"You work hard?" Blumboum asked, his voice gruff but direct. His gaze, sharp and assessing, lingered on the thin, nervous Vietnamese boy standing before him, clutching his worn hat. He watched for any sign of hesitation, any flicker of weakness.

Minh, understanding the crucial importance of the moment, nodded eagerly, almost too eagerly. "Yes, sir. I work hard. Very hard," he stammered, his limited English making his earnestness all the more poignant.

Blumboum's lips barely curled into what could be called a half-smile. "Good. I pay you fifty cents per hour. Cash. No taxes." His words were clipped, final, leaving no room for negotiation or questions. Without a word, he pointed to the sink.

Minh didn't know what the legal minimum wage was in this state, in this country. He didn't know he was being egregiously underpaid, exploited because of his vulnerability and desperate circumstances. He only knew, with a profound sense of relief, that three dollars for a six-hour shift was infinitely better than nothing at all. It was money, real money, for his family: money for food, for rent, for the very necessities of their fragile new beginning. He bowed deeply, his head bent in a gesture of profound gratitude, murmuring his thanks to Mr. Blumboum for the opportunity that, in his eyes, was a lifeline thrown to a drowning man. He didn't yet know the true cost of that lifeline.

Long Hours, Empty Pockets

The job was brutal. Every shift was a relentless grind, a twelve-hour marathon that stretched from the moment the restaurant doors swung open for the breakfast rush until the last dish was scrubbed clean and stacked high in the dead of night. There was no designated break, not even a quick five minutes to catch his breath, and certainly no offer of a free meal, despite the tantalizing aromas that constantly wafted from the kitchen. It was just the ceaseless, deafening clang of dishes, the biting sting of scalding water on his skin, and the dull ache in his back and arms.

Sometimes, Mr. Blumboum, the bulky owner with the sharp eyes, would demand extra tasks from Minh. "You do it, Minh. You want to work, don't you?" he'd say with a wide, knowing grin that never quite reached his eyes, his voice thick with oily condescension. These tasks always took him outside of his dishwashing duties: sweeping the vast, greasy parking lot under the scorching sun, unloading heavy flour sacks and crates of produce, or clumsily trying to fix wobbly chairs in the dining area. Minh always said yes. He had to.

One blustery night, long after the last customer had left and the restaurant lights had dimmed, Minh sat hunched outside on an overturned crate, utterly exhausted, waiting for his ride home. The cold bit at his exposed skin, but he was too tired to shiver. Lisa, a kind-faced waitress with tired eyes, came out for a smoke. The glow of her cigarette was a small, fleeting beacon in the darkness. She looked at him, her gaze softening with unmistakable pity.

"You know he's ripping you off, right?" she said, her voice low and laced with concern.

Minh blinked, his exhausted mind struggling to grasp the unfamiliar idiom. "Ripping?" he mumbled, his voice hoarse.

"Cheating you," she clarified, taking another drag. "He's supposed to pay at least a dollar fifty an hour. That's the minimum wage. And you should definitely be getting breaks, legally. He can't just work you straight for twelve hours." Minh didn't know what to say. The words hung heavy in the cold air between them, undeniable and suffocating. He knew, instinctively, that she was right, but the truth didn't offer comfort. He needed this job. He needed the money, every single, hard-earned coin, for May, for his younger siblings, for their fragile foothold in this new world.

Lisa sighed, the smoke curling from her lips. "He does this to all the new immigrants," she continued, her voice thick with weary resignation. "Pays you under the table, works you like a dog, and pockets the extra cash. He knows you won't complain because you're desperate, and you won't report him."

Minh swallowed hard, a bitter lump rising in his throat. His fists clenched involuntarily, but his head remained bowed, his gaze fixed on the cracked pavement. He thought about his mother, May, her tired but hopeful eyes. He thought about his hungry siblings, their small faces depending on him. He couldn't risk losing this job. Not for anything.

So he said nothing. The silence stretched between them, thick with unspoken understanding and the harsh reality of his situation.

The Cost of Survival

Months bled into more months. The seasons changed outside, but Minh's routine remained unyielding, a cycle of grueling labor and weary slumber. He saved every dollar he could, carefully stashing it away and contributing every cent to his family's meager household. He never once asked for a raise, nor did he complain when Mr. Blumboum, with casual cruelty, threw yet another unexpected, unpaid task his way. The restaurant owner, a master of exploitation, continued to make a fortune off Minh's silent, tireless labor, long, uncompensated hours, no benefits, and absolutely no complaints. For Blumboum, Minh was the perfect employee.

One sweltering afternoon, as Minh wiped down tables in the nearly empty dining room, his movements slow with fatigue, he overheard Blumboum talking loudly to another local businessman at the cashier's counter.

"Best workers you'll ever find," Blumboum boasted, a coarse laugh rumbling in his chest. "They never ask for more, never take breaks. Just happy to be here, happy to have a chance. I've got this kid, Minh, washing dishes for less than what I'd pay some high school dropout. It's a damn goldmine!" His words, sharp and demeaning, cut through the quiet air like shards of glass.

Minh's fists clenched tightly at his sides, nails digging into his palms, but he kept his head down, wiping the same spot on the table over and over, pretending he hadn't heard a single word. In that moment, a harsh, undeniable truth solidified within him. He had learned something profound and bitter about America. It was indeed a land of opportunity, a place where dreams were supposedly born. But he realized, with chilling clarity, that this opportunity wasn't always, or equally, extended to people like him: immigrants, refugees, those with nowhere else to turn.

Still, he kept working. He kept scrubbing. He kept enduring. Because he had no other choice. Because he now understood, with a heavy heart, that survival always came at a profound and often unseen price.

The Night of Demons

One chilly October night, the darkness had already fallen outside, and Minh was still at work. As the wind howled like a hungry, unseen beast, rattling the thin windows of their small apartment, May's family hoped for a peaceful evening. The world beyond their walls, wrapped in the deepening autumn dusk, was still profoundly unfamiliar, filled with bewildering customs and unspoken rules. But inside their modest home, they found comfort in each other's quiet presence. The soft, amber glow of a single lamp cast long, dancing shadows across the walls, creating an illusion of safety and warmth, a fragile cocoon against the vast unknown.

A sudden, sharp knock at the door shattered the silence, making everyone jump in startled surprise. Chi, usually the most outgoing of the younger children, pushed herself up from the floor where she had been engrossed in a drawing. Her small hand reached for the cold doorknob. As she cracked open the door, a sliver of porch light cutting into the dim room, her eyes widened in horror.

Standing outside, half-shrouded in the dim, swirling light, were strange, eerie figures, some with faces painted a ghastly, unnatural green, their features distorted and menacing; others had eyes that seemed to glow with an otherworldly luminescence. They were draped in dark, flowing cloaks that billowed in the October breeze, topped with bizarre, pointed hats that defied earthly explanation.

Chi let out a strangled gasp, a sound that was half-scream, half-sob, choked back by terror. With a surge of primal instinct, she slammed the door shut with a resounding thud, pressing her small back against it, as if to physically bar the grotesque creatures from entering. Her feet felt frozen to the ground, rooted by an unshakable fear that left her utterly immobile.

"MAMA!" she shrieked, her voice raw, laced with panic. "There are witches at the door! They've come for us! They've found us!" Before May could process Chi's frantic words, Khanh, always impulsive, rushed forward. He yanked the door open just a crack, his face contorting in fear as he caught a quick, horrified glimpse of the figures outside. A shocked yelp escaped him, quickly stifled as he slammed the door shut again with desperate force. His face was pale, mirroring the stark terror in Chi's wide eyes.

May, heart pounding, felt a mixture of maternal protectiveness and creeping dread. Cautiously, she approached the fortified door. Trembling, she pulled aside the curtain on the narrow window next to it and stole a fearful glance outside. Her breath hitched in her throat as icy dread formed a cold knot in her stomach. It was real, the Devil himself, or something equally malevolent, stood at their door, surrounded by a demonic entourage, cloaked in shadows. With a startled gasp, she instinctively jumped back, a chill creeping up her spine, a sensation she hadn't felt so acutely since their frantic escape from their homeland.

But May immediately sprang into action. Her motherly instincts, honed by years of protecting her children through unimaginable dangers, took over with fierce resolve. Her face, though pale, was set with determination. She swiftly gathered the children into the cramped living room. "Stay together!" she commanded, her voice firm and resolute. "Pray loudly! Pray for our safety, children!"

The children, pale and streaked with tears but resolute in their faith, clutched hands together, their fingers interlaced. They formed a small, united circle of hope, chanting prayers with voices that rose in a chaotic but determined chorus, a mix of pure fear and fervent devotion, a desperate plea for divine protection against the evil at their doorstep.

Outside, the confused "witches", who were actually just a group of boisterous neighborhood kids in elaborate Halloween costumes, stood bewildered by the sudden, shrieking uproar from inside the quiet apartment. Their initial delight at possibly scaring someone had quickly dissolved into genuine confusion. A little boy, his face painted a ghastly white with fake blood dripping from his lips as a vampire, tugged on the sheet-draped arm of his friend, who was dressed as a ghost. "Why are they screaming in there?" he whispered, his voice muffled by his plastic fangs. "Did we scare them that badly? What did we do?"

Finally, a kind neighbor, having overheard the commotion next door, came to investigate and, thankfully, explain the misunderstanding. Laughing gently, her voice warm and reassuring, she approached the terrified apartment door and knocked softly, with a different, less menacing rhythm. "It's okay!" she called out, her words cutting through the lingering tension. "Don't be afraid! It's Halloween! They're just kids asking for candy!"

When May hesitantly peeked through the curtains again, her eyes wide with lingering suspicion, she saw the children on the porch, not with menacing claws or glowing eyes, but holding out small, innocent, pumpkin-shaped buckets. A profound sigh of relief escaped her lips, and the rigid tension in her body slowly, almost visibly, receded, leaving her limbs weak and trembling.

"No witches?" Chi asked nervously, her voice still a tiny whisper, as she clung tightly to May's leg, her small face etched with doubt.

"No witches," the neighbor chuckled warmly, her laughter echoing the relief now spreading through the small family. "Just Trick-or-Treaters, sweetie. They want treats!"

Realizing the cultural misunderstanding, the family, still slightly shaken but now immensely relieved, burst into a collective peal of laughter. It was a sound of cathartic release, a mix of embarrassment at their exaggerated fear and genuine amusement at the absurdity of the situation.

That night, amidst the lingering scent of autumn and the fading echoes of their own fearful prayers, they learned about Halloween, a strange, bewildering, but ultimately harmless and joyful American tradition of playful frights and sweet treats. By the next year, fully prepared and now embracing their place in the community, they were ready.

Their apartment glowed with welcoming lights, and they had a big, overflowing bowl of candy, making sure no other new, bewildered family would ever have to pray away Trick-or-Treaters again.

Learning a New Language

As the initial shock of their arrival softened and the echoes of their first bewildering encounters faded, life began to settle into a new, more structured, and undeniably purposeful rhythm. The church, a steadfast pillar of support in their new, sprawling community, recognized a fundamental need and quickly initiated a formal English class, an essential lifeline for the new arrivals. Held twice a week, on crisp Tuesday and Thursday evenings, these classes transformed a small, utilitarian room near the main church building into a vibrant hub of learning. Usually used for Sunday school, the space now hummed with quiet concentration.

Volunteers, an eclectic, dedicated group of retired teachers, college students, and compassionate community members, sat patiently with the refugees, often for hours. They used simple, brightly colored flashcards, illustrated storybooks meant for children but helpful for learners of all ages, and engaging games like "Simon Says" and "I Spy" to teach the basics of English. The air was often filled with the soft murmur of new words being attempted, corrected, and mastered.

"Hello." "My name is May." "How are you?" "Thank you very much." These were the foundational stones, the first sounds of a new language that May practiced tirelessly.

May approached these lessons with an unwavering dedication that shone in her eyes. She carried a small, well-worn English textbook, its pages filled with neat, unfamiliar characters, and practiced every day, often late into the night after the children had gone to sleep. Her accent was thick, a melodic echo of her homeland clinging stubbornly to each new word, but her determination was thicker still, a quiet, unyielding force that propelled her forward. She carefully copied new words and phrases into a small, spiral-bound notebook, transforming it into a tangible record of her progress.

At dinner, around their small, borrowed table, she turned the lessons into a family activity, quizzing the children on pronunciation and meaning, reinforcing their learning while strengthening her own. Sometimes, the children, who grasped the new sounds more easily, would laugh at her pronunciation. Their laughter, innocent and light, broke the intensity of the day. May laughed too, a soft, genuine chuckle. Then, with a playful but firm glint in her eye, she'd make them repeat the word three times correctly, ensuring they solidified their understanding and cultivated respect for the new language.

Beyond classroom instruction, the church provided practical, tangible assistance, serving as a crucial bridge to their integration into the bustling, sometimes overwhelming, new society. These were not just lessons, but lifelines.

They found Minh, the responsible eldest son, a part-time job washing dishes at a busy local diner. It was grueling work, the air thick with the scent of fried food and dish soap, his hands perpetually wet, but it was his first paid job in America. It offered him a taste of independence and a necessary step toward contributing to his family's new life, despite the long hours and physical demands.

They also helped Hoang sign up for after-school tutoring, recognizing his quiet eagerness to learn and his bright potential. The extra support he received helped bridge the educational gap, giving him the tools to succeed in the unfamiliar American academic environment.

One particularly kind woman, Mrs. Lewis, a beacon of practical wisdom, brought over a stack of colorful sewing patterns and patiently taught May how to use a sewing machine. The hum and whir of the machine were new sounds, but the rhythmic motion was oddly comforting. "You can make clothes for your family or fix them when they tear," Mrs. Lewis explained with a gentle, encouraging voice. "Or maybe even sell them, if you get good enough, May. There's always a need for good needlework."

It was a simple suggestion, casually offered, but in May's heart, it sparked a quiet, hopeful idea of self-sufficiency, a path to not just survive but perhaps even thrive creatively and economically in this bewildering new world.

Hoang's Job

Hoang's job, though different from Minh's back-breaking labor, was arguably no less brutal, perhaps even more insidious in its daily humiliations. He worked as a janitor at a local high school, a massive, echoing building that never truly seemed to sleep. His duties were endless and thankless: mopping seemingly infinite stretches of linoleum floors until they gleamed, hauling overflowing trash bins that reeked of forgotten lunches and teenage carelessness, and, worst of all, cleaning the public bathrooms. These were not just quick swipes; they often bore the marks of deliberate vandalism and cruel pranks.

Some of the girls, teenagers themselves, wielding their newfound power with chilling malice, knew Hoang was shy, quiet, and unfamiliar with the nuances of American culture and its unwritten social rules. They deliberately, almost gleefully, stuffed sanitary pads into the toilets, watching from a calculated distance. Their high-pitched laughter echoed off the tiled walls, their faces alight with cruel amusement as they observed his embarrassment and struggle to unclog the overflowing mess. The sight of his confusion, his mortified attempts to fix something he barely understood, brought them perverse joy. Each incident chipped away at his dignity, leaving him feeling exposed and utterly alone.

Despite this profound humiliation, this constant erosion of his self-worth, Hoang knew with a steel conviction deep in his bones that he had to keep working. He had to endure this daily torment to support his beloved siblings, to ensure their survival and stability in this bewildering new world. He couldn't afford the luxury of quitting, of walking away from the meager but essential paycheck. To save every possible penny, he stubbornly refused to take the school bus, even on the coldest, most unforgiving mornings or the sweltering, humid afternoons. Instead, he walked.

The long walk home, a grueling several miles through the biting cold of winter or under the scorching, relentless summer sun, became his only escape, his sanctuary. It was during these walks that Hoang allowed himself a few private minutes, a sacred sliver of time just for himself. In these stolen moments, away from prying eyes and the demands of his day, he let the suffocating weight of anger and embarrassment surface. He replayed the incidents in his mind, the cruel giggles of the girls, the contemptuous stares, the profound sense of helplessness. Each heavy, rhythmic step felt like dragging the immeasurable weight of his shame, exhaustion, and loneliness behind him. Some days, his legs ached so badly, the muscles burning with fatigue, that he wanted nothing more than to collapse on the cracked pavement, to give in to the overwhelming physical and emotional burden. But he forced himself forward, one painful step after another, his will stronger than his weariness. He clenched his fists at his sides, his nails digging crescent moons into his palms, desperately trying to swallow the bitter, suffocating anger boiling inside him, a hot, acrid taste in his mouth.

The worst days were when his eyes burned with unshed tears, a searing sensation that threatened to betray his carefully constructed composure. On those days, he had to bite his lip so hard it sometimes bled, just to keep the tears from falling. He didn't want anyone, not a passing stranger, not his family, not even the cruel girls at school, to see him like that. Crying, to him, meant weakness, vulnerability, and exposure. He had no room, no capacity, for weakness in this unforgiving reality. So, he walked, staring fixedly at the ground, his gaze glued to the shifting patterns of dirt and cracks, his mind filled with a tumultuous storm of thoughts he could never dare to say out loud. The sheer, crushing unfairness of it all, how they had survived a brutal war, endured unimaginable horrors, only to end up scrubbing floors and being cruelly laughed at for their cultural ignorance, ate away at him relentlessly, dissolving his spirit like corrosive acid. But there was no choice, no other path. He had to keep going. He had to endure. For his family. Always for his family.

Duy Flees

One chilly evening, as the last rays of an autumn sun faded from the window, the May family gathered around their small, somewhat rickety dinner table after a long, exhausting day. The familiar clatter of bowls and the comforting aroma of rice and stir-fried vegetables filled the modest apartment. Duy and Long, fresh from their new American school, sat happily munching on their food, their youthful energy slowly replenishing. But as May watched them, her keen maternal eye caught something odd, a subtle, repetitive motion that immediately piqued her suspicion. Both boys kept reaching up, their fingers raking through their hair, constantly, almost unconsciously.

May narrowed her eyes, a familiar flicker of concern turning to suspicion. "Why do you keep scratching?" she asked, her voice tinged with a knowing sharpness, her gaze fixed intently on them.

Duy and Long exchanged quick, nervous glances, a silent, guilty communication passing between them before shrugging with forced nonchalance. "It's just itchy, Má," Long mumbled, avoiding her gaze, his voice lacking conviction.

May wasn't convinced, not for a second. With the swiftness of a mother who had seen it all, she reached across the table, grabbed Long's head firmly but gently, and with practiced fingers, parted his thick dark hair. What she saw made her gasp, a sharp, choked sound of disbelief and dismay. "Trời đất ơi! Lice!" she exclaimed, the Vietnamese phrase for "Oh my goodness!" bursting from her lips, a mixture of shock and exasperation. The tiny, insidious creatures, unmistakable, crawled visibly along his scalp.

Minh, sitting nearby, absorbed in his own meal, nearly choked on his rice, sputtering in disbelief. "What? Lice? Here? In America?" he spluttered, the idea seemingly impossible in this new, supposedly clean and orderly country.

Without hesitation, May, fueled by a sudden surge of determination, grabbed Duy's head next. Her inspection was swift and decisive. Same problem. Her youngest son, too, was infested. She stood up so fast her cheap kitchen chair nearly toppled over with a screech. "No good! No good! You two, bathroom! Now!" she commanded, her voice firm and non-negotiable.

The boys barely had time to protest, their half-eaten dinners forgotten, before May marched them sternly to the tiny, linoleum-floored bathroom. Her movements were quick and efficient as she rummaged through the small, cluttered cabinets beneath the sink, searching desperately for a solution. Shampoo? No, not strong enough. Bar soap? Useless. Her eyes darted around, a growing desperation in her expression, until they landed on a large, industrial-looking can of bug spray sitting on the kitchen counter, left there perhaps by the landlord for ant control. It was definitely not meant for human use, let alone for children's delicate scalps, but May wasn't about to let tiny, persistent American bugs defeat her. Not after everything they had survived.

With grim determination etched on her face, she grabbed the can. Her resolve was absolute. She pulled the bewildered boys into the small, porcelain bathtub, its cold surface a stark contrast to their warm bodies, and swiftly covered their faces with a towel. "Close your eyes, don't breathe!" she ordered, her voice sharp, leaving no room for argument, before giving their heads a thorough, unsparing dousing with the potent spray. The strong, acrid chemical smell instantly filled the cramped bathroom, burning their nostrils and making Duy and Long cough reflexively, their small bodies tensing.

After what felt like an eternity, but was only a few minutes, May scrubbed their heads clean with vigorous, almost violent motions, rinsing away the foamy residue and the now-dead lice. Then, she checked again, her fingers meticulously combing through their still-damp hair. Success! The lice were gone, eradicated by her unconventional, but undeniably effective, method. She nodded proudly, a small, triumphant smile gracing her lips. "See? American lice, Vietnamese mom. Mom wins," she declared, a quiet victory in her ongoing battle with the challenges of their new life.

However, as Duy's hair slowly dried in the cool air of the bathroom, something strange and unexpected happened. His normally smooth, perfectly flat, dark hair, which had always lain straight against his scalp, began to stiffen and curl in odd, unruly directions, springing out stubbornly. No matter how much he combed it, trying to flatten it, or wet it down again, it refused to lie flat, instead forming a wild, unmanageable halo around his small head. Long, with his naturally thick and more resilient hair, seemed miraculously unaffected by the chemical assault, but poor Duy, his hair remained a frizzy, wiry, defiant mess for an entire, agonizing year, a testament to May's desperate, well-intentioned, but ultimately hair-altering solution.

Every morning before school, Duy would stand in front of their small, smudged mirror, his eyes burning with frustration, and glare at his unruly reflection. "Má, look at my hair!" he would groan, his voice a mix of exasperation and despair. "I look like a scared chicken!" The comparison was apt; his hair did indeed stand on end in startled, wiry clumps.

May would simply wave him off, dismissing his woes with a practical, unyielding logic. "Better scared chicken than lice farm, con," she'd reply, her voice firm. And in her mind, that was the undeniable truth.

The Day Chi Took Baby Ngoc to School

It began on a deceptively quiet Sunday afternoon. The sky overhead was a vast, clear canvas of unbroken blue, and the gentle warmth of the fading autumn sun filtered through the apartment window. Inside, the comforting sounds of May cooking in the kitchen, the rhythmic chop of vegetables, the sizzling of oil, filled the air, creating a rare moment of domestic calm. On the surface, everything seemed to be in perfect, serene order.

But not for May. Beneath her outward composure, her mind buzzed with a growing undercurrent of anxiety. She had a profoundly important meeting scheduled for the very next morning, a formal gathering organized by the U.S. government specifically for the Vietnamese refugee community. It was an event of great significance, where stern-faced officials would be present, delivering solemn speeches, guiding them through daunting paperwork, and engaging in serious, often intimidating discussions about their new lives. There would be coffee in flimsy paper cups and an atmosphere of weighty bureaucracy. Definitely not the kind of place for a baby.

And yet, there was Baby Ngoc, May's youngest and most spirited child, plump and undeniably adorable, right in the middle of the living room floor. Ngoc was happily, obliviously chewing on a discarded sock, completely absorbed in her discovery, shrieking with sudden bursts of pure, unadulterated delight every few minutes, her joyful cries echoing through the small space.

May glanced anxiously at the worn clock on the wall, its hands ticking away the precious hours. Her heart sank. No babysitter. No daycare. Not a single neighbor she felt comfortable enough to ask for such a significant favor, not yet. The older children, including Chi, would all be in school, immersed in their own new, challenging routines.

Time was mercilessly running out, pressing down on her like a heavy weight.

Then, a flicker of an idea ignited in her mind. It was a strange, desperate, and certainly unconventional idea, born from sheer necessity.

She turned slowly, deliberately, to Chi, her eldest daughter, who was quietly engrossed in a worn library book, its pages dog-eared from frequent reading.

"You will take Ngoc to school tomorrow," May said, her voice firm and resolute, leaving no room for argument, even as the words felt audacious.

Chi looked up from her book, her eyes, usually so astute and intelligent, wide with a mixture of disbelief and utter shock. She pointed a trembling finger first to herself, then to the happily babbling baby Ngoc, her silent question palpable. "Me?"

May simply nodded, a slow, determined affirmation. There was no other way.

Chi stared for a long, agonizing moment, her gaze sweeping from her mother's unwavering expression to the innocent, sock-chewing baby. Then, a profound sigh escaped her lips, a sound of resigned acceptance to the impossible task ahead.

Monday Morning

The next morning dawned crisp and cool, a typical autumn day, as Chi walked slowly toward the imposing brick building of the elementary school. Her arms were held carefully, almost protectively, clutching a thick, patterned blanket. Underneath its soft folds, Baby Ngoc was warm, delightfully soft, and wiggling gently, like a contented kitten nestled in a basket. The baby's rhythmic breathing was the only sound.

Chi kept her head bowed low, her gaze fixed on the cracked pavement, her shoulders hunched slightly as she moved with exaggerated care, trying her best not to draw any attention to her unusually precious cargo. Every hurried step she took was an attempt to remain invisible.

Ngoc, miraculously, was calm at first. In the first class, a muffled hum of unfamiliar English words, she slept soundly, her tiny chest rising and falling with peaceful regularity. Chi held her gently but firmly, positioned strategically in the very back row of desks, shrouded by the desk itself, her heart pounding a nervous rhythm against her ribs. She didn't understand much of what the teacher said, the words a dizzying blur of sounds, but she understood one thing perfectly, with a clarity that transcended language:

Don't let the baby be seen. Don't let anyone know.

In the second class, just as Chi felt a cautious sense of relief beginning to settle over her, Ngoc began to stir. Her small body stretched, a tiny, almost imperceptible movement under the blanket. Then, she made a little trumpet sound with her mouth, a soft, inquisitive pffft, and blinked her big, innocent eyes up at Chi, ready to engage with the world.

Chi's heart leaped into her throat. She coughed loudly, a strained, theatrical hack, hoping to cover the sound. Her cheeks flushed crimson.

A boy in the row in front of her, curiosity piqued, turned around, his eyes narrowed. "What was that?" he asked, a hint of suspicion in his voice.

Chi just shook her head, a quick, dismissive gesture. The boy, still frowning, raised his eyebrows in a quizzical expression, then, mercifully, turned back to face the front of the classroom, his attention shifting.

Third Period: Disaster

The fragile peace was shattered in the third period. It began subtly, with a tiny, almost imperceptible squeal from beneath the blanket, quickly followed by a soft, gurgling sound.

Then, the blanket itself began to twitch violently. A small, chubby foot, clad in a tiny pink sock, kicked free, triumphantly emerging into the open air.

Then came the smell.

It was faint at first, a subtle shift in the classroom's air, but it quickly grew stronger, a distinctly pungent, undeniable odor.

Chi's eyes widened in profound, mortified understanding. She looked down in horror. Ngoc was red-faced, her cheeks puffed out, grunting softly with effort, happily kicking her legs with unbridled joy, utterly unaware of the catastrophe she was unleashing. The smell grew stronger, thickening in the air. It crept through the unsuspecting classroom like an unstoppable fog, slow, insidious, and utterly pervasive.

A girl in the front row, whose nose was usually upturned with an air of superior disdain, wrinkled it sharply.

"Do you smell that?" she whispered loudly to her friend, her voice laced with disgust.

A boy in the middle row leaned back in his chair, sniffed dramatically, and groaned, a theatrical sound of pure revulsion. "Ugh! What is that? It smells like... like rotten milk and baby farts!"

The teacher, Mrs. Jenkins, who had been meticulously writing a complex math problem on the chalkboard, paused mid-stroke. Her brow furrowed in a deep frown. She slowly turned, her gaze sweeping across the classroom, searching for the source of the burgeoning disturbance. "What is going on here? What is that terrible smell?" she asked, her voice sharp with irritation.

Chi froze, utterly paralyzed. Her face burned with humiliation. She didn't need to understand every single English word. The incredulous, disgusted, and suddenly very interested faces around her said more than enough. Their stares felt like physical blows.

The blanket shifted again, vigorously. Baby Ngoc, emboldened by her successful escape from partial concealment, peeked out with a grand flourish, her chubby face beaming. She gave the entire stunned class a proud, toothless smile and then, with surprising volume, shouted,

"BAAAAH!"

The room went completely silent. A heavy, charged stillness fell over the students, broken only by the persistent, undeniable aroma.

Then,

Chaos. Screams of surprise and disgust. Bursts of uncontrollable laughter, loud and mocking. Chairs scraping loudly against the floor as students scrambled to get away from the source of the stench.

A boy in the front row pointed a shaking finger directly at Chi and shrieked, his voice cracking with excitement and disbelief, "THERE'S A BABY! CHI HAS A BABY!"

The teacher, Mrs. Jenkins, blinked slowly, her jaw slack with confusion, as if someone had indeed brought an actual farm animal into her meticulously ordered classroom. "Miss... Chi?" she said cautiously, her voice a strained whisper, as if she were confronting an optical illusion. "Is that... a child? In your arms?"

Chi, her face burning even deeper crimson, stood up quickly, clutching the smelly, giggling baby Ngoc close to her chest. Without a word, her dignity shredded but her resolve firm, she walked briskly, almost running, toward the hallway, the baby's happy gurgles trailing behind her.

The class sat in stunned, bewildered silence, the previous pandemonium replaced by a quiet awe. The teacher opened her mouth to say something, anything, but then, seeing the full scale of the bizarre situation, she simply gave up, letting her mouth fall shut with a soft click.

The unmistakable smell of baby poop followed Chi out the door like it belonged there, an invisible, fragrant cloud of defeat. Later That Day

By the time May arrived to pick them up, the late afternoon sun casting long shadows across the schoolyard, Chi was sitting quietly in the antiseptic-smelling front office. She held a sleepy, miraculously clean Baby Ngoc, who was now contentedly sucking her thumb. Chi stared off into the middle distance, her eyes unfocused, and her posture stiff and weary, like a young soldier returning from a harrowing, unseen battle.

The diaper bag, which May had meticulously packed that morning, was now conspicuously half-empty. One of Chi's school uniform sleeves was covered in a white, powdery residue of baby powder, a futile attempt to mask the earlier disaster. Her school bag, clutched tightly in her lap, had a distinct, mashed banana stain smeared proudly on its front. Each detail told a story.

The principal, a stern-faced woman with tightly pulled-back hair, handed May a long, neatly folded note. It was filled with official-looking English words that May couldn't fully understand, a dense paragraph about school policy, unexpected visitors, and appropriate conduct. But she understood enough. The principal's pursed lips and the tone of her voice conveyed the unspoken message: this cannot happen again.

May, her expression unreadable, scooped up Ngoc, who immediately brightened, smiling like she was immensely proud of herself, utterly oblivious to the chaos she had caused. The baby squealed with unbridled joy, reaching out chubby hands to grab May's necklace, delighted to be reunited with her mother.

Chi stood up slowly, her movements stiff and tired, as if every joint ached. She quietly handed her mother the now-pristine baby blanket, her eyes downcast. She said nothing. Not a word of complaint, not a single explanation. She didn't have to. Her face, a picture of profound exhaustion and unspoken trauma, said everything: Never again. Never, ever again.

May looked at her eldest daughter, a mix of gratitude, understanding, and a touch of sorrow in her eyes. She gave Chi a kind, gentle smile, a small comfort in the aftermath.

"You did very well, con," May said softly, using the Vietnamese term of endearment. "Everyone loves babies."

Chi didn't reply. She just turned and walked outside with slow, tired, almost shuffling steps, her shoulders slumped, her eyes half-closed, her young spirit weighed down, like someone who had truly lived through something no child ever should have to endure.

The Apple Harvest and the Big Barbecue

As the seasons flowed and transformed, marking the passage of time in the vast, serene landscapes of Idaho, May and her family slowly, painstakingly adapted to their challenging new life. Each changing leaf, each snowfall and thaw, brought with it a deeper understanding of this foreign land. With the arrival of autumn came the apple harvest, a time not only of back-breaking labor but also, unexpectedly, of deep community spirit and communal celebration.

One crisp, sun-drenched day, a local farmer named Mr. Johns, a tall, broad-shouldered man with a perpetually warm, crinkling smile and hands deeply roughened and calloused by decades of working the rich, unforgiving earth, met Minh at the bustling church outreach center. Mr. Johns had long admired the family's quiet determination, observing from a distance how they persevered with unwavering resilience despite the daunting language barrier and the harsh, often unforgiving Idaho winters. Moved by their dignity and quiet strength, Mr. Johns kindly extended a generous offer to Minh: a temporary, much-needed job helping with the demanding apple harvest.

"Bring your family along," he said, his voice kindly gruff, a genuine warmth in his eyes. "Harvesting apples is always more fun and goes faster when you do it together. There's plenty of work for everyone." His invitation was more than just a job; it was an unspoken gesture of welcome.

The Exciting Day of the Apple Harvest

On the crisp, dew-kissed morning of the harvest, May and her children woke long before the sun had fully crested the eastern hills, the pre-dawn air biting with a delightful chill. They layered on every warm piece of clothing they owned, bundling themselves against the brisk autumn air before setting off on their purposeful walk toward Mr. John's vast, sprawling orchard. The air around them was thick with the intoxicating, sweet scent of ripe apples, damp, fertile earth, and the distant, invigorating aroma of pine forests. Row upon row, the apple trees stood, their sturdy branches heavy, almost burdened, with an abundance of vibrant red and glistening golden fruit, bending gracefully under the sheer weight of the impending harvest. The children, their eyes wide with unrestrained excitement and anticipation, burst ahead, their breath puffing out in visible, playful clouds in the chilly morning air, their laughter already echoing through the quiet orchard.

Minh and Hoang, with their youthful strength and quick learning, were swiftly instructed in the proper, gentle technique to twist the apples off the branches without causing any damage to the delicate fruit or the precious trees. The younger girls, Phuong, Khanh, and Sang, armed with smaller, manageable baskets, giggled with delight as they picked what they could reach from the lower branches, their laughter bubbling up whenever an apple, missed or dropped, fell with a soft, satisfying thud onto the cushioned grass below. May, meanwhile, worked steadily, her hands moving with swift, practiced grace, her movements economical and efficient. Now and then, Mr. Johns would walk by, his presence a comforting reassurance, nodding in silent approval at their tireless efforts.

Phuong and Sang's eyes widened even further, sparkling with unadulterated joy, when they were later given their own, larger, empty baskets, not for work, but to collect apples from the trees that still had luscious fruit clinging to their uppermost branches. They didn't have to pick them for the commercial harvest; they were gathering them purely for fun, for the sheer joy of it. Their basket grew heavy quickly,

156

filling with their eager, small hands. When they finally reached the central pile of harvested fruit, they tumbled over themselves, giggling wildly as they proudly showed off their harvest to their mother.

"Look, Mama, so many!" Sang exclaimed, her small voice bursting with pride, even though her collected apples were a bit crooked, some slightly bruised, and none as perfectly formed as the ones picked for market. May smiled, a profound, tender emotion swelling in her heart, a mixture of love and pride that threatened to spill over. For a fleeting, precious moment, it felt like they were just like any other family in this new country, laughing together, sharing a simple, uncomplicated joy under the vast Idaho sky.

As the sun climbed higher, casting longer, warmer rays over the orchard, Mr. Johns' kind-faced wife arrived, carrying a large, steaming thermos of hot apple cider and a platter piled high with fresh, still-warm cinnamon rolls, their sweet aroma mingling with the scent of the apples. She smiled warmly as she handed a steaming cup of the spiced drink to May, who hesitated for a brief moment, unaccustomed to such overt kindness, before accepting it with a heartfelt nod of gratitude.

"You're doing great, May," Mrs. Johns said gently, her voice soft and encouraging. "Hard work always deserves a good reward. Please, enjoy." Her words, simple yet profound, wrapped May in a comforting blanket of acceptance.

By the time noon arrived, their arms aching from the cumulative effort but their spirits high and buoyant, they had filled countless sturdy wooden crates with apples, their bounty a testament to their collective labor. The orchard, once heavily laden with crimson and gold, now looked perceptibly lighter, the trees visibly relieved of their sweet burden, standing taller and straighter in the afternoon light.

The Barbecue Celebration

That very evening, as twilight painted the sky in hues of orange and purple, Mr. Johns extended a warm, heartfelt invitation for the family to join a grand barbecue celebration at his sprawling farmhouse. The intoxicating scent of grilled meat, juicy burgers and savory sausages, mingled with the sweet, earthy aroma of roasted corn, filling the cool evening air as people from all corners of the small town gathered, their voices a cheerful murmur of chatting and laughter. Long, rustic tables were set under the vast, open sky, draped with cheerfully checkered tablecloths and charmingly decorated with plump pumpkins and baskets overflowing with the day's freshly picked apples. Lanterns strung between trees cast a warm, inviting glow.

May, usually reserved and quietly observant in social settings, found herself relaxing as she watched her children run freely, their boundless energy uncontained, playing spirited games with the farmer's rosy-cheeked grandchildren. Minh, ever responsible, gravitated towards the large, smoky grill, helping Mr. Johns flip burgers with practiced ease, the sizzle of meat a background rhythm. Hoang, his shyness slowly receding, found a comfortable spot with a group of local teenagers, Mr. Johns' nephew among them, slowly but surely picking up more and more English words, his vocabulary expanding with every shared joke and casual conversation. Phuong, Khanh, and Sang, their eyes wide with wonder and delight, sat eagerly with other children, their small hands clutching pieces of their very first taste of homemade apple pie, a warm, sweet, spicy revelation.

At one point, as the laughter and chatter briefly subsided, Mr. Johns raised a glass, his eyes sweeping across the diverse gathering. "To May and her family," he announced, his voice ringing with genuine sincerity. "Welcome to Idaho. Their hard work and resilience, coupled with the kindness of our community, truly shine through. We are honored to have you."

May, not understanding all the English words, felt the profound warmth in his voice, the sincerity of his gaze, and the collective goodwill emanating from the gathered faces. She stood up slowly, gracefully, placing a hand over her heart, and bowed deeply, a gesture of deep humility and heartfelt thanks that transcended any language barrier. "Cảm ơn," she said softly, her voice thick with emotion, then translated, "Thank you. Thank you very much."

As the barbecue continued into the gentle embrace of the evening, the unburdened laughter of the children became the soundtrack of the night. Phuong and Sang, their faces bright with sheer excitement, ran around the vast farmyard, their joyful screams echoing under the canopy of the setting sun, playing a spirited game of tag with Mr. Johns' young grandchildren. They darted through the tall, rustling grass, their movements swift and light. Every time one of them was caught, they would collapse into a heap of giggling limbs, rolling on the soft, cool ground, their infectious mirth spreading through the air.

Minh, who had been diligently focused on helping with the grill, his face smudged with charcoal, found his serious demeanor cracking under the onslaught of pure, childish joy. He couldn't resist joining in. Tossing a couple of perfectly grilled burgers onto a nearby table, he quickly sprinted after the younger kids, his long legs covering ground effortlessly. With his youthful speed, he was clearly faster than the little ones, but he pretended to be slow, deliberately fumbling and stumbling, so the younger ones could have the thrill of catching him. Hoang, feeling increasingly comfortable with her improving English skills, sat with Mr. Johns' nephew and a small group of other teenagers about her age, all chatting and laughing easily as they tried to make conversation about school, music, and local life.

Now and then, Hoang would glance over at the younger children, a soft smile on his face, watching them play happily, their innocent giggles truly filling the cool, clear air.

The night came to a gentle, serene close beneath a sky scattered with an impossibly vast tapestry of shimmering stars, their soft, distant light dancing across the dark canvas above. Around a crackling bonfire, its flames reaching eagerly towards the heavens, warmth radiated outward into the cool night air, its golden light flickering across familiar, smiling faces. Laughter, bright and unburdened by past sorrows, rang out frequently as the children played nearby, their joy pure and unfiltered, a testament to newfound happiness.

May sat quietly on a wooden bench, wrapped in a borrowed blanket, watching them all with a heart full of wonder and a quiet, profound sense of peace. For so long, she had carried the heavy, relentless weight of fear, uncertainty, and constant struggle. But here, in this luminous circle of light and kindness, surrounded by warmth and acceptance, that immense burden slowly, almost imperceptibly, began to lift from her shoulders. They were no longer just strangers in a cold, unfamiliar place, constantly on guard.

Her children had made real friends, companions who welcomed them without hesitation, who shared their games and laughter, their simple joys of childhood. And May, too, had found a deep, unexpected connection in the warmth of open-hearted conversation, in the simple gestures of care that didn't ask for anything in return, only offered.

They weren't just surviving anymore. They were, finally, beginning to belong.

In that precious moment, surrounded by the comforting warmth of the bonfire, the genuine friendship of their new community, and the soft hum of burgeoning hope, May knew with a certainty that settled deep in her soul: they had found more than just safety. They had found a home.

Chapter 23

Decision to Move to California

Life, gradually but persistently, settled into a more discernible and somewhat predictable rhythm for May and her family in Idaho. The initial raw edges of displacement began to soften, giving way to the mundane realities of daily existence. Minh, with his quiet determination, found new work at a different local restaurant, a bustling diner a few towns over, where he tirelessly brought home whatever small earnings he could to bolster their meager household. His hands were still perpetually chapped, but the work felt a little less oppressive than before.

Hoang, now a diligent high school student, poured himself into his studies with almost fervent intensity, determined to carve out a better, more dignified future for himself and his family, recognizing education as their strongest tool. The younger children, both the boisterous boys and the ever-curious girls, attended school too, diligently learning English, their accents slowly softening, and gradually adjusting to the bewildering customs and rhythms of their unfamiliar new world.

Yet, no matter how busy and demanding the weeks became, how many challenges they faced, Sundays always belonged, exclusively and undeniably, to May. Before the first hint of dawn each Sunday morning, she would gently, meticulously wake the children, ensuring they were dressed warmly and ready for church. Rain or shine, bitter cold or sweltering heat, even through the biting Idaho snow, the five-mile walk to the church was never in question. It was her sacred ritual, her lifeline, her way of anchoring the family in unwavering faith, constantly reminding them that they were part of something larger than themselves. This spiritual community transcended their immediate struggles.

As the years passed, marked by the growth of children and subtle shifts in their understanding of America, the Vietnamese community across the United States began to grow stronger, more organized, and more vocal. A Vietnamese radio station, a true marvel, emerged, its signals reaching across vast distances to broadcast news, traditional music, and heartwarming stories specifically tailored for Vietnamese immigrants scattered across the country. The familiar voices, the melancholic melodies from home, and the comforting cadence of their native tongue drifted through the family's small apartment, a nostalgic balm that made the immense distance from Vietnam feel just a little less vast, a little less painful.

Then, one fateful day, May heard something on the radio that made her heart unexpectedly race , a frantic flutter in her chest, a segment discussing how many Vietnamese families were actively resettling in Southern California. The mere possibility of joining a thriving, established Vietnamese community, of reconnecting with others from her cherished homeland, of speaking her language freely outside her home, lit a powerful, incandescent spark inside her. It was a vision of belonging she hadn't dared to dream of since their chaotic arrival.

Change, a force they knew intimately, was stirring once again, but this time, it felt different. It felt like hope.

Without hesitation, driven by this sudden, profound revelation, May called Minh and Hoang to sit down with her at the kitchen table, their faces still etched with the weariness of their long days.

"We are moving to Southern California," she announced, her voice steady and resolute, filled with an unshakeable certainty that brooked no argument. Her eyes, usually soft, now held a glint of absolute conviction.

165

Minh and Hoang exchanged startled glances, their surprise palpable. "Moving? But why now, Má?" Minh asked carefully, trying to understand this abrupt, monumental decision after all they had built here. "We've finally settled."

May crossed her arms over her chest, her posture firm. "Because the Vietnamese community is growing there, strong and vibrant. It will mean better chances for all of us, more opportunity for work, for education, for life. More people like us. We won't have to be strangers forever in this country, always feeling so alone." Her gaze held a mixture of fierce love and practical foresight.

She fixed them both with an unwavering gaze, her eyes piercing theirs. "You two will go first. You will buy a car, drive to California, and find a place for us. Then, when you are settled, you will come back, and we'll move the whole family, all of us together." It was an order, a directive given with absolute authority and trust.

Minh nodded thoughtfully, his mind already, instinctively, mapping out the daunting steps ahead, the logistics of such a journey. Hoang, though undeniably surprised by the suddenness and scale of the plan, knew better than to challenge their mother when her mind was so clearly made up. He understood the unspoken strength behind her decision.

When May made up her mind, it was never a question of if it would happen, only when, and how swiftly. Her will was the family's compass.

The Red Chariot to California

May's directive had been clear, delivered with the unshakeable certainty of a matriarch mapping destiny: Minh and Hoang were to go first. Their mission was to acquire a car, drive it to California, and secure a new home for the family. The very idea of it, navigating the sprawling American highways in a vehicle they hadn't yet purchased, felt both exhilarating and terrifying. Their collective funds were meager; a tight knot of savings painstakingly accumulated from Minh's underpaid dishwashing and Hoang's janitorial wages. A new, reliable car was a distant dream, a luxury beyond their wildest imagination. An old car, however, a reliable-enough clunker, was within the realm of possibility.

Their search began the very next morning, armed with a crumpled newspaper classified section and a small, worn phrasebook. They walked to every dusty used car lot within bus distance, past gleaming sedans and imposing trucks, until their eyes landed on it: a glorious, faded old red

167

Ford van. It wasn't just red; it was a defiant, sun-bleached cherry stain, streaked with years of Idaho dirt and fading memories of brighter days. Its fenders sported dents that told silent tales of forgotten encounters with mailboxes or errant fence posts, and one headlight was slightly askew, giving it a perpetually surprised expression. But it stood there, proud and sturdy, a silent sentinel amidst a collection of less fortunate automotive brethren.

The salesman, a wiry man named "Slim" who wore a perpetually skeptical grin and chewed on an unlit cigar, sauntered over, clearly sizing them up. He began his practiced spiel, a rapid-fire torrent of English words about "dependability" and "classic American muscle," none of which Minh and Hoang fully grasped.

"This beauty here," Slim declared, slapping the Ford's hood with a hollow clang, "she's got good bones! Runs like a dream! A steal at, uh, five hundred bucks!" He quoted a price that made Minh's heart sink like a stone.

Minh, summoning every English phrase he knew, pointed to the dented fender. "Uh, bonk," he managed, making a clumsy hitting motion. Then he pointed at the askew headlight and mimed a look of confusion. "Light... boop?"

Slim chuckled, a dry, raspy sound. "Ah, just a little character, son! Adds personality! And that light, just needs a good whack, usually pops right in!" He demonstrated with a theatrical tap that had absolutely no effect.

Hoang, ever the more practical one, circumvented the aesthetic discussion. He opened the driver's door, which groaned in protest, and pointed to the ignition. "Start? Vroom-vroom?" he asked, making a hopeful engine sound.

Slim, surprised by their directness, reluctantly handed them the keys. "Sure, go on, take her for a spin. You'll see."

Minh carefully started the car. The engine coughed twice, then sputtered to life with a rumble that sounded less like a "vroom-vroom" and more like an elderly bear clearing its throat. Smoke, a somewhat concerning shade of bluish-gray, puffed from the exhaust pipe. They drove it slowly around the block, the steering wheel a bit loose, the brakes making a faint, high-pitched protest. It was far from perfect, but it was a step in the right direction. It drove.

Back at the lot, Slim leaned against the Ford, flicking his cigar. "So, boys? What do you say? Best darn car you'll find for under a grand!"

Minh, remembering May's strict budget, held up three fingers. "Three... hundred... dollars." He enunciated each word slowly, clearly, his voice firm.

Slim's jaw dropped, and he choked on his phantom cigar. "Three hundred?! Are you kidding me? This is a classic!" He puffed up, ready for a long, drawn-out negotiation.

But Minh and Hoang stood there, their expressions unyielding, their faces blank. They had made their offer. They had no other offer. Their silence spoke volumes, a powerful counterpoint to Slim's bluster.

Slim paced for a moment, eyeing the old Ford, then the two earnest young men. He knew this car had been sitting here for months, a rusty monument to lost hope. "Alright, alright!" he threw his hands up in mock surrender. "You boys drive a hard bargain! Three hundred! But you gotta promise to tell your friends where you got such a great deal!" He winked, already calculating his meager profit.

Minh and Hoang exchanged a quick, triumphant glance. Three hundred dollars! They had done it! They had purchased a car, a venerable, albeit battered, old red Ford that, by some miracle, still ran. It was a far cry from a modern vehicle, its interior smelling faintly of dust and forgotten French fries, its suspension groaning over every pothole. But it had wheels, an engine, and enough space for their family and their meager belongings. For them, it wasn't just a car; it was a red chariot, a symbol of their daring escape and their journey towards a new, hopefully brighter, future in California. They had bought a car for so little money, a deal that, in their eyes, was nothing short of miraculous.

A New Sun

Minh and Hoang had returned from their intrepid scouting trip to Southern California, their old red Ford now a veteran of the open road. They had successfully moved the entire family down from the chilly plains of Idaho. The transition was immediate and profound. The California weather was nothing like the biting cold and harsh winters they had endured in Idaho. Here, the air didn't sting at their skin or freeze the inside of their nose. Instead, it wrapped around their backs in a gentle, persistent warmth, a comforting embrace that felt like a healing balm after years of shivering. It touched their faces like the tender caress of an old, long-lost friend.

May stood on the sun-drenched sidewalk outside their modest new apartment in Orange, near Chapman University, the vibrant heart of their new city. She listened intently to the steady hum of distant traffic, a metropolitan symphony, mingling with the joyful, uninhibited sound of children's laughter. It was a melody woven harmoniously in both rapid-fire English and the familiar, comforting cadence of Vietnamese. The younger children, having absorbed English with remarkable ease and speed, now spoke it far more fluently, their accents almost imperceptible, bringing a fresh, dynamic energy to the familiar warmth of their home. Her world, once shattered into countless, terrifying fragments by war and displacement, was beginning to heal, piece by painstaking piece, under the glow of this new sun.

Here, in Southern California, the Vietnamese community was not just present; it was thriving, pulsating with vibrant life and cultural authenticity. Bustling markets overflowed with exotic produce and familiar delicacies, their aromas transporting May back to the marketplaces of her youth. Cozy noodle shops, their windows steamed with savory vapors, offered the comfort of traditional phở and bún bò Huế. And a church, a haven for their faith and culture, stood just a short, reassuring walk away. It was a place where they could effortlessly meet more Vietnamese people, finding familiar faces and common stories. They could purchase things that had once been impossibly scarce: essential spices for authentic cooking, fresh herbs, and traditional clothing. In a truly profound way, it felt as though a small, cherished piece of Vietnam had somehow traveled with them across oceans and continents, bringing an undeniable sense of comfort, connection, and belonging to their new, still-evolving life.

A year had passed since their arrival in Southern California, a year filled with rapid adjustments and quiet triumphs. The kids were adapting to their new environment in ways that often surprised even themselves, shedding their old fears and embracing new possibilities. Hoang, whose determination was as strong as his intellect, had picked up English with such astonishing speed that he now spoke faster than even Minh or Chi, his words flowing effortlessly. Long, the more outgoing of the middle children, had made close, genuine friends at school, finding a true sense of belonging and camaraderie in his new environment. Sang, with her strong will and particular tastes, still stubbornly refused to eat soft, bland American sandwiches. Still, she had warmed considerably to her favorite teacher, who affectionately called her "Sunshine," a nickname that brought a rare smile to Sang's face.

Then there was Ngoc, now a curious and boisterous four-year-old. She was... well, uniquely herself. She understood Vietnamese perfectly, responding to every command and question with knowing nods and bright smiles. Yet, to May's constant bewilderment and exasperation, she would only answer in English. No matter how many times May asked her something in Vietnamese, gently coaxing or playfully commanding, Ngoc would look at her with an impish grin and respond in flawless, confident English, as if her mother hadn't even uttered a single word in the other language. It was as if she'd made a silent, steadfast decision: once you're in America, you're all in, no exceptions, no holding back. May couldn't help but laugh at her youngest daughter's stubborn determination, even if it drove her a little crazy, a tangible manifestation of their full immersion in their lives.

One quiet evening, as May meticulously unpacked the last of their boxes, carefully arranging their meager possessions in their new, sparsely furnished apartment, her fingers brushed against something soft. She pulled it out: an old, cherished photo, its colors faded to sepia tones, the edges softly curled from years of transit and careful handling, a poignant relic from Vietnam. It was her husband, his smile captured forever in time. She gazed at the image for a long, silent moment, a wave of bittersweet memories washing over her, before gently, reverently, tucking it between the pages of a well-worn book on her nightstand, a secret solace. That night, sleep wouldn't come easily. The California air felt too warm, too still, and her heart felt too heavy, too full, overflowing with a complex blend of grief, gratitude, and a fragile, burgeoning hope.

Outside, the faint, melodic sound of a car radio drifted through her open window, playing an old American love song, its wistful melody echoing the quiet emotions in her heart. May sat by the window, gazing up at the vast expanse of stars, a celestial tapestry familiar yet profoundly changed.

We made it, she thought, a quiet whisper in the stillness of the night. But we're not done. Not yet.

Home Sweet Home

Every morning in their new California life, May woke before the first blush of dawn, the apartment still cool and quiet. Her day began with the comforting rituals of home: preparing bowls of fragrant rice porridge or assembling savory bánh mì sandwiches for breakfast, their scent filling the small kitchen. Afterward, she would sit by the window, a serene silhouette against the burgeoning light, carefully watering her small pots of precious herbs, vibrant green basil, delicate purple-veined perilla leaves, and fragrant, slender stalks of lemongrass. These tiny patches of green were her direct connection to the earth of her homeland. The girls, dutiful and quiet, helped her meticulously clean the apartment before rushing off to

175

school, while the boys, Minh and Hoang, packed their books and were out the door with youthful urgency, eager for their pursuits.

Minh and Hoang, now young men shouldering significant responsibilities, worked long, demanding hours. Minh, with his growing confidence and experience, had found a steady job at a local auto body shop, his hands now perpetually stained with grease and oil, but his pockets no longer empty. Hoang, balancing ambition with necessity, continued his college education in the evenings, diligently pursuing his dreams while working part-time at a bustling grocery store, where he bagged groceries and stocked shelves. At night, gathered around the table, they would share stories of their day, their voices softened by fatigue, over steaming bowls of canh chua, a comforting Vietnamese sweet-and-sour soup, and generous portions of rice. The simple meal was a symbol of their unity. They would laugh softly, truly grateful just to be together, safe, and building a life.

Long and Duy, the younger boys, spent their afternoons riding bikes with carefree abandon through the quiet, sun-dappled streets of Orange, their laughter echoing through the suburban lanes. On weekends, they actively helped May at the bustling flea markets, where she had established a small, popular stall. She proudly sold her homemade delicacies: crispy, golden egg rolls, fragrant sticky rice wrapped in banana leaves, and vibrant, sun-dried fruits. May, with a newfound sense of independence and self-reliance, adamantly refused to accept charity now. "We're in America," she would often say, her voice firm, her gaze resolute. "We build with our own hands. This is our way."

Over time, through countless hours of hard work and careful scrimping, the family saved, bit by bit, dollar by dollar, each coin a testament to their perseverance. May kept a thick, worn envelope of cash hidden deep within her kitchen drawer, wrapped securely in an old, faded scarf. Her mistrust of traditional banks ran deep, an unhealed scar from her tumultuous past in Vietnam, where she had witnessed firsthand how easily savings could disappear, swallowed by war or corruption. The vivid, painful memories of those difficult, unpredictable times made her profoundly hesitant to rely on formal institutions, and she preferred, unequivocally, to keep her hard-earned money close, where she felt she had direct control, where she could physically touch it and know it was safe.

One bright spring afternoon, Minh came home, the daily newspaper clutched in his hand, his face alight with an almost boyish excitement, a rare sight that immediately caught May's attention. He handed the paper to May, his finger tracing a small, unassuming advertisement he had circled in bright red ink. It was for a modest, four-bedroom house for sale right there in the city of Orange. The house itself wasn't anything extravagant, its exterior was plain, its paint slightly peeling, but it immediately caught Minh's imaginative eye. It had a backyard, a rare and precious feature in their compact, urban life, a space where the children could play freely.

There were a couple of mature olive trees, a vibrant orange tree, and a promising lemon tree, a poignant, living reminder of the fruit trees they'd been forced to leave behind in their ancestral village in Vietnam. And crucially, there was a small, unkempt garden space, just big enough to grow a few essential vegetables, something that resonated deeply with May, where growing your own food had always been a fundamental way of life, a connection to the earth. For a powerful, hopeful moment, the simple newspaper ad felt like a tangible glimpse into a future that could finally feel permanent, truly theirs.

"It's nothing fancy, Má," Minh said softly, his voice tinged with a hopeful reverence, "but it's ours if we want it."

May studied the faded photo of the house for a long, silent moment, her fingers lingering at the edges of the newsprint, imagining. Then, with careful, deliberate movements, she folded it and tucked it gently beneath the scarf in her secret drawer, among her precious savings.

"Call them," she said quietly, her voice barely a whisper, yet firm with unspoken resolve. "Let's see it."

The entire family visited the house the following Sunday, a pilgrimage of sorts. It needed work, the kitchen tiles were chipped in places, the paint on the walls was dull, and the garage door groaned ominously when opened, but May walked through the rooms as if they were already sacred, imbued with future memories. She didn't just see empty rooms; she saw her grandchildren there already, their laughter echoing as they ran across the living room, chasing bubbles in the sunlit yard.

With the compassionate guidance of a kind Vietnamese-American realtor, who understood their unique journey, and a small, crucial loan co-signed by Minh, they made the down payment a month later. May brought the envelope of cash to the realtor's office herself, clutching it tight against her chest as if it might disappear into thin air, a lifetime of sacrifice held precariously in her hands.

When the papers were finally signed, the last ink still wet, and the heavy set of keys officially handed over, May walked outside. She stood quietly in the front yard, a slight breeze rustling her hair, and stared up at the laden lemon tree. Its branches swayed gently, heavy with bright, ripening fruit, a symbol of abundance and new beginnings.

"We're home," she whispered, the words a soft, heartfelt prayer, a declaration of a long-sought peace.

Home Sweet Home

With the family fully settled into their new house, each room beginning to resonate with the echoes of their presence, life started to bloom in subtle, comforting ways. The process of making the house a home began almost immediately, piece by painstaking piece, as they brought in furniture and prepared for their very first American holiday under their own roof.

A mere week after they received the keys, a large, generous sofa arrived, a gift from a local church group. It was a behemoth of a couch, with faded green fabric that bore the marks of many past lives, and a spring that let out a distinct, almost musical squeak whenever anyone sat down too fast or shifted their weight. Yet, to May, it wasn't just a used sofa; it was a grand, comfortable throne, a symbol of stability and belonging.

Bit by precious bit, the house began to fill with other mismatched but dearly cherished pieces of furniture: a sturdy dining table acquired from a kind neighbor who was downsizing, its surface already bearing the faint rings of countless shared meals. A set of practical bunk beds, bought second-hand from a bustling garage sale, quickly became the source of whispered secrets and playful wrestling matches for the boys. Even a clunky, old television found its way into their living room, rescued from a curb by Hoang and meticulously fixed by his clever hands, its screen flickering to life with grainy images of American sitcoms and news. Every single item had a story, a testament to their resourcefulness and the generosity of their new community, and every piece carried an immeasurable weight of gratitude.

May, with her quiet strength, found immense joy in the most minor, most intimate details of creating their sanctuary. She spent hours lining drawers with cheerful floral paper, a touch of unexpected beauty. She folded towels with meticulous precision, just so, and carefully placed a beloved photo of her husband, whose colors had softly faded with time, on the mantel in a simple wooden frame. "You would be proud," she whispered to the picture one quiet morning, her voice thick with emotion, a silent communion across continents and realms. "They've grown into good, strong young men who are respectful, hardworking, and full of purpose. And our girls are blossoming, too."

Soon, the crisp days of November arrived, and with it, the quintessentially American holiday of Thanksgiving. May didn't quite grasp the concept of the holiday at first; it was another cultural enigma. But the children, now fluent in American customs, patiently explained it: it was a time to give thanks, to gather around a bountiful meal, and, most importantly, to be with family. That part, the essence of gratitude and togetherness, she understood deeply, for it resonated with the core values of her heritage.

They decided to embrace both worlds, blending traditions. Their Thanksgiving feast would feature both a grand, traditional American roasted turkey and May's special, aromatic phở, its steaming broth rich with hidden flavors. Minh, ever the eager learner, insisted on taking charge of roasting the turkey, diligently poring over recipes in a borrowed American cookbook, determined to master the art of the golden bird. Hoang, with his newfound culinary confidence, handled the mashed potatoes, laughing heartily as he inevitably spilled milk on the counter. The girls, their fingers nimble and creative, decorated the house with handmade paper leaves in autumn colors and small, flickering candles, casting a warm glow. Duy and Long, a

182

mischievous duo, worked together to string twinkling lights along the front porch, transforming their humble entrance into a festive welcome.

That evening, as the perfectly roasted golden bird emerged from the oven, filling the entire house with its rich, savory aroma, the fragrant steam rose from May's giant, bubbling pot of phở on the stove, the new house felt full, full of tantalizing smells, full of joyful sounds, full of vibrant life.

They all sat together at the long dining table for the very first time in their own new home, a moment of profound significance. It didn't matter that the chairs were a mismatched collection, each a different style and height, or that some of the plates were chipped along the edges. What mattered was their shared presence. Minh, his eyes shining with pride and emotion, raised his glass of sparkling apple cider. "To the past we survived," he declared, his voice firm, "and to the future we build, here, together."

May's eyes welled with tears, reflecting the flickering candlelight, and she nodded silently, her heart overflowing with a gratitude too deep for words.

Later that night, as the family curled up in their now-furnished, comforting rooms, the sounds of the day settling into a gentle hum, Long whispered to Duy from the bunk above, his voice soft with wonder, "This is the first real home I remember, Duy. The first one that feels like it's ours."

Duy didn't answer right away, a profound thought lingering. Then he said, his voice equally hushed, "Me too."

And for the first time in many years, perhaps truly for the first time in their young lives, they all slept not just with full stomachs and tired bodies, but with hearts overflowing with a peace that felt like home.

May's First Job

A few weeks after that memorable Thanksgiving, with the festive glow still lingering, May, fueled by a renewed sense of purpose, began her daily quest for employment. Each morning, she would set out on foot, systematically stopping at every small Vietnamese shop and bustling restaurant tucked away in the vibrant strip malls of Bolsa, the heart of Little Saigon. Her eyes, earnest and unwavering, spoke what her limited English words could not: I will work hard. Please, give me a chance. I need this.

One fortunate day, her persistence paid off. A small, bustling Vietnamese-owned bakery in Bolsa, its air thick with the sweet aroma of freshly baked goods and coffee, welcomed her in. The owner, a kind, soft-spoken widow named Bà Lan, whose hands were dusted with flour but whose eyes held a sharp, knowing gaze, offered May a job folding countless delicate pastry boxes and helping with basic prep work in the warm, fragrant kitchen. It paid little, barely enough to cover a few groceries, but it was honest, dignified work. May never arrived late, never left early, always performing her duties with quiet diligence. Without fail, she always brought home leftover pastries, flaky croissants, sweet bread, and airy cream puffs, a special treat for her children, their faces lighting up with delight at the unexpected indulgence.

On Sundays, with the same unwavering devotion, she still gathered the kids, their newly pressed clothes rustling, and walked to church, this time, however, the familiar ritual unfolded beneath the majestic, swaying fronds of palm trees, their shadows dancing on the sidewalk, a stark, comforting contrast to the biting Idaho snows they had once endured.

Hoang, the driven and quiet scholar, struggled more than the others with the social nuances of their new life. High school was harder now, not just academically, but socially. The American kids talked fast, their slang a bewildering code. They dressed in expensive, fashionable clothes he couldn't possibly afford, and made jokes whose cultural references he didn't understand, leaving him feeling perpetually on the outside. After school, he worked diligently as a busboy at a local phở restaurant, clearing tables and scrubbing floors, his uniform smelling faintly of beef broth. Then, late into the night, long after his siblings were asleep, he would stay up at the kitchen table, hunched over his textbooks, a worn English-Vietnamese dictionary his constant companion, painstakingly translating his homework word by word, syllable by agonizing syllable.

One night, May found him asleep at the table, utterly collapsed from exhaustion, his young face resting on his open textbook, a pen still clutched loosely in his hand. Her heart ached with a mother's profound empathy. She didn't wake him, choosing instead to let him rest.

Instead, she gently draped a soft blanket over his slumped shoulders, her touch light as a feather, and whispered, "Cố lên, con trai. You're doing more than enough." The Vietnamese phrase, meaning "Try hard, my son" or "Hang in there," was a silent benediction, a recognition of his immense sacrifice and unwavering effort.

Meanwhile, Long and Duy, with the boundless creativity of childhood, had built a vivid world of their own, a fragile sanctuary tucked between the ordinary realities of their new life and the wild expanses of their imagination. After school, they constructed elaborate forts from discarded cardboard boxes found behind grocery stores, their architectural masterpieces rising from alleys and vacant lots. They sped through the quiet, sun-dappled alleyways on battered bikes, their tires squealing, their voices weaving a joyous, unintelligible hybrid of English and Vietnamese, a secret language that belonged only to them, a testament to their unique bicultural existence. One quiet afternoon, as May worked in the kitchen, she heard their voices drift through the open window, carried on the gentle breeze.

Duy: "Long, when we grow up, we'll be heroes, right?"

Long: "Yeah. We'll save people. Like the man who pulled us out of the water when the sea snake came. This time, we'll save him too. We won't lose his knife, and we're definitely not going to Australia."

Their boisterous laughter echoed down the street as they pedaled furiously away, their imaginations already carrying them on their next grand adventure.

Love in the Air

It was a bright, impeccably clear Sunday morning in Orange, California, and, as always, May had everyone up early and meticulously dressed for church. Five years in

America had brought countless changes. Still, her Sunday routine remained an unyielding constant: her áo dài (traditional Vietnamese dress) neatly ironed, her hair tied back in a tidy bun, and a thermos of hot tea packed in the car "just in case someone faints" from the heat or the long service, a pragmatic concern rooted in her long-ago past.

Chi, now twenty, vibrant and sharp-witted, had stopped arguing about the rigid Sunday schedule years ago. She slipped into her modest dress, a comfortable compromise between tradition and her growing American identity, and begrudgingly got into the car with her siblings. Church wasn't so bad, she conceded. It was always a lively event, half traditional Catholic Mass, half vibrant Vietnamese potluck. She genuinely liked seeing her friends, and perhaps even more, she appreciated that the "aunties" always brought something delicious to eat: sticky rice wrapped in banana leaves or savory grilled nem chua.

That morning, however, something was subtly... different. While standing by the folding chairs after service, chatting idly with Phuong, Chi noticed a young man helping to set up tables in the bustling church courtyard. He was tall, with a gentle, somewhat shy face, and he was clearly trying his best to fit in, but the way he carefully, almost awkwardly, unwrapped the delicate rice paper for spring rolls and hesitated before passing out the plates made it painfully obvious: he was new. Very new to California.

May noticed, too, of course. She leaned in conspiratorially, a knowing glint in her eye, and whispered, "He's fresh in California, con. I can smell the fish sauce on him from here." Then, her expression softening into a thoughtful assessment, she added, "But he's handsome. He reminds me of your Ba (father) when we first met, except your Ba had better pants."

The young man, seemingly drawn by an invisible thread, introduced himself during the food line, his voice a little hesitant. His name was Huy. He had only come to California a few months ago after spending years in a desolate refugee camp in the Philippines, a purgatory of waiting. His English was still rough, accented by years of hardship, but his smile was honest, radiating a quiet sincerity. He helped wash dishes after the meal, diligently scrubbing alongside the other volunteers, and when the pastor asked for more volunteers to stay and clean up the entire hall, he didn't hesitate for a moment, raising his hand immediately. That's when May, seeing his immediate willingness to serve, leaned over to Chi again and whispered, her tone laced with approval, "That one is not lazy. That is a good sign."

189

Later that day, as the afternoon sun began its slow descent, Huy's uncle, a respectable elder in the community, approached May respectfully, speaking in the old village way, his words steeped in tradition. "Sister May," he began, his voice polite and deferential, "my nephew, Huy, is a very sincere young man. He saw your daughter, Chi, today. He found her very beautiful and kind... he would like permission to get to know her better, if it pleases you."

May gave a tight-lipped smile, a blend of traditional reserve and modern maternal protectiveness, and nodded slowly. "Let me ask her first," she replied, her eyes betraying nothing.

When Huy and his uncle had finally departed, Chi immediately burst into raucous laughter with her siblings, unable to contain her mirth. "Did you see his pants?" she gasped, wiping tears of laughter from her eyes. "I swear, he looks like a scarecrow that wandered out of an Idaho cornfield and ended up at a Vietnamese potluck! And that belt! It was practically strangling him!"

Phuong cackled loudly, Duy snorted soda out of his nose, and Long, ever the witty one, said, "That poor guy's belt was working overtime trying to hold those things up!"

But May wasn't laughing. Her expression was solemn, her eyes fixed on Chi with a long, unblinking look.

"Don't laugh at him, daughter," she said calmly, her voice carrying an unexpected weight of wisdom. "That boy has heart. A good heart. In this country, decent, hardworking men like that are not easy to find. You mark my words."

Chi tried to shrug off her mother's words, a casual gesture, but something in her mom's unwavering tone, a hint of steel beneath the softness, made her glance back out the window, just in time to see Huy, still smiling gently, bow slightly as he climbed into his uncle's car. There was a quiet dignity about him, even in his ill-fitting clothes.

Later that night, as Chi changed into her pajamas and prepared for bed, she noticed something odd on her small nightstand. That same boy, Huy, had folded a delicate paper crane from a church bulletin, its creases sharp and precise, and left it on the table. Her name was written neatly on its wing, in both flowing Vietnamese script and blocky English letters.

She stared at the tiny origami bird for a long moment, a strange mixture of surprise and something akin to a blush rising in her cheeks. Then, without a word to anyone, she carefully tucked it into her worn journal, a new secret.

May, standing at the kitchen sink, washing the last dishes of the day, caught the moment out of the corner of her eye. She didn't say anything either, just a small, knowing smile played on her lips. She whispered to herself, "Đấy, mới có một con hạc giấy mà nó mềm lòng rồi." (See? Just one paper crane and her heart's already melting.)

The next Sunday, Chi told herself she wasn't looking for anyone in particular, certainly not a boy with questionable fashion sense. But before leaving, she applied a subtle layer of lip gloss "because it's not a sin," tied her hair back with a vibrant red ribbon, and, in a rare deviation from her usual habit, even took her jacket off before walking into church, allowing her modest dress to be seen.

The service felt exceptionally long, longer than usual, probably because Father Nguyễn was on one of his legendary storytelling sprees, weaving tales that stretched on and on. But during the final hymn, as the congregation's voices swelled, Chi couldn't help but glance up. And there he was again. Huy. Standing quietly in the back row, his shirt buttoned all the way to the top like a proper, old-fashioned church boy, his hair a little less shiny with product than last week, but his smile still just as sincere, perhaps even a little more hopeful.

After the final prayer, when the service officially ended, Huy was one of the first to step forward, eagerly helping to move the folding chairs, his movements quick and efficient. This time, Chi didn't run off to hide in the kitchen or join her siblings. She lingered nearby, pretending to meticulously search for a misplaced spoon in the large box of shared utensils, her ears straining to catch any sound from him.

Suddenly, a voice, a little nervous but determined, spoke directly behind her. "You like nước mắm with everything too?"

She turned, genuinely surprised, her heart giving a little flutter. It was Huy, holding a plate laden with rice and grilled chicken. He looked nervous, his eyes darting, like he'd been practicing that line all morning, steeling himself for the approach.

Chi raised an eyebrow, a flicker of her usual playful sarcasm. "Of course. If it doesn't smell like old socks, it's not real nước mắm." (She explained later in her mind: it's a traditional Vietnamese fish sauce made by fermenting fish (usually anchovies) with salt, a staple condiment known for its deep umami flavor, saltiness, and distinct aroma.)

Huy blinked, absorbing her unexpected reply, then burst into genuine, unrestrained laughter. "Yes! I tell people here, but they don't understand! They say 'smells too strong!'" His laughter was warm, infectious, a relief.

Chi grinned, a real, unforced smile. "You're not from here. You from Saigon?"

He shook his head, still smiling. "No, I'm from Biên Hòa. Small place. But now... here is home, I think." His gaze met hers, holding a silent question.

They stood there for a comfortable moment, side by side, holding their plates, letting the easy conversation stretch between them as the noisy courtyard faded into the background.

Then, amidst all the surrounding chatter and laughter, Chi said softly, impulsively, "Sorry about what I said last week."

Huy tilted his head, genuinely confused. "What you say?" he asked, his brow furrowed slightly.

Chi hesitated, then laughed, a light, genuine sound. "Never mind. Your pants look better this week."

He smiled, still a little confused by the odd compliment, but clearly happy that she had spoken to him again. Then, with a practiced, smooth movement, he reached into his jacket pocket and pulled out another perfectly folded paper crane, this one crafted from a church donation envelope, its colors more muted. "For you," he said, offering it to her. "Next week, I'll learn how to fold a flower. I think you like flowers more."

Chi took it, her fingers brushing his lightly. She tried not to smile too much, instead keeping her expression cool and casual. "You better," she challenged playfully. "I like flowers more than birds."

From across the courtyard, May stood next to a tray of bánh bèo (steamed rice cakes), pretending to be deeply engrossed in conversation with an old friend. But her eyes never left her daughter. She saw the way Chi now leaned a little closer to Huy, the subtle tilt of her head. She saw the way Chi didn't roll her eyes when he spoke, a habit May knew so well.

May sipped her tea slowly, a small, knowing smile playing on her lips. She nodded once, a silent affirmation, and whispered to herself, "Đấy, mới có một con hạc giấy mà nó mềm lòng rồi." (See? Just one paper crane and her heart's already melting.)

Permission or Interrogation?

Huy had navigated countless formidable challenges in his young life, the abrupt abandonment of his promising law degree in Saigon when the brutal war forced his desperate flight from Vietnam, the arduous, solitary journey of learning English from scratch, one painstaking word at a time, and the grueling, humble beginnings of his first job in America, scrubbing cars at a noisy car wash. Yet, none of those formidable obstacles, none of those personal trials, truly compared to the sheer, stomach-churning terror he was about to face: asking Mrs. May, the formidable matriarch of the household, for her sacred permission to date her cherished daughter, Chi.

He had dressed meticulously for the occasion, choosing his absolute best button-up shirt, a crisp, pale blue garment that still smelled faintly of fabric softener. There was no trace of hair gel this time, he deliberately wanted to project an image of humility and earnestness, certainly not slickness or superficiality. In one hand, he clutched a pastel pink box of delicate pandan waffles from a reputable Vietnamese bakery, their subtle, sweet aroma a comforting presence. In the other, he held a small, neatly tied bag of glistening dried persimmons, their deep orange hues hinting at a natural sweetness. His wise old uncle had always, absolutely always, impressed upon him that bringing fruit, especially dried fruit, was a time-honored symbol of deep respect and genuine sincerity in Vietnamese culture. He prayed, with every fiber of his being, that this ancient wisdom held true, even in modern America.

May was in the kitchen when he finally gained the courage to approach, her back to him, her hands moving with the dizzying speed and precision of a culinary ninja, deftly cutting vibrant green onions into impossibly thin, perfect rings. The air in the house was a rich tapestry of pungent, authentic aromas: the sharp, unmistakable tang of fish sauce, the pungent bite of garlic, and, to Huy's heightened senses, an almost palpable scent of impending judgment.

Huy bowed slightly, respectfully, his heart thumping against his ribs. "Ma'am," he began, his voice a little shaky but steady, "I have something I'd like to talk to you about, if you have a moment."

She didn't even look up, her hands continuing their rhythmic dance with the green onions. "Go ahead, Huy. I'm listening," she said, her voice even, revealing nothing. The sound of her knife against the cutting board was the only reply.

Chi, meanwhile, had conveniently vanished upstairs, presumably "doing homework," a flimsy excuse that fooled no one, least of all Huy. He knew, with absolute certainty, that she was pressed against the banister, eavesdropping with both ears, every word amplified by her nervous anticipation.

He cleared his throat, the sound dry and nervous. "I… um… I would like to humbly ask your permission to get to know Chi better. Respectfully," he managed, adding the crucial, polite qualifier.

May finally ceased her chopping, the knife resting silently on the board. She slowly turned, her eyes, usually soft and maternal, now sharp and piercing like a hawk's, directly pinning him in place. "Get to know her, huh?" she echoed, a hint of suspicion in her tone. "What exactly are you trying to find out, young man? Her blood type? Her glasses prescription? Her social security number?" She folded her arms, her gaze unblinking.

She sighed deeply, a long, drawn-out sound that seemed to fill the entire kitchen, and then, with deliberate slowness, she stood up from the counter. She walked toward him, her movements measured and commanding, like a seasoned general inspecting a new, untested recruit, assessing every nuance.

"You love your mom?" she asked, her voice low, direct.

"Yes, ma'am," Huy replied, his posture ramrod straight.

"You treat your sister with respect?"

"Yes, ma'am. Always."

She paused, her gaze unwavering, then leaned in close, her voice dropping to a low, intense whisper that sent a shiver down Huy's spine. "You make my daughter cry... I'll make you cry louder. Understand?"

Huy straightened even further, meeting her gaze head-on. "Yes, ma'am. I understand completely."

May studied him for a moment longer, her keen eyes searching his face for any hint of deceit or weakness. Then, with an unexpected, almost playful gesture, she gave him a light slap on the back, gentle enough not to hurt, but firm enough to make him blink in surprise.

"Good boy. You're not scared. That's a good start," she declared, a rare, fleeting smile gracing her lips.

Then, just as quickly, she walked away, returning to her green onions, mumbling under her breath, "He's sweet... but he's not done being tested yet. Not by a long shot."

A moment later, Chi tiptoed into the kitchen, a picture of innocent distraction, pretending with exaggerated nonchalance that she hadn't been listening to every single word. "Well?" she asked, her eyes wide and feigning ignorance.

Huy grinned, a mixture of relief and genuine amusement washing over his face. "I think your mom just threatened me, Chi."

Chi smirked, a knowing glint in her eyes. "Then congratulations, Huy. You've been officially accepted into the family."

The Dinner Test

When May, with her typical blend of quiet authority and grand hospitality, said, "Let's invite him over for dinner," she didn't mean a casual, thrown-together meal. Oh no. She suggested a full-on, Tết-level, break-out-the-good-rice-cooker, all-hands-on-deck kind of evening. It was to be a culinary spectacle, a traditional Vietnamese feast, an actual test of character disguised as a simple supper.

Huy was formally invited for 6 p.m. In classic Vietnamese fashion, meant to show utmost respect and eagerness, he showed up at 5:30. In Vietnamese culture, this could indeed be seen as a profound mark of deep respect and enthusiasm, or, as May's initial reaction proved, a total, unmitigated disaster if the kitchen wasn't in a state of absolute readiness.

May was still in her apron, stained with the day's culinary battles, her sleeves pushed up to her elbows, her long, dark hair pulled into a quick, hastily tied knot that had already begun to unravel in the heat and humidity of the kitchen. Strands clung stubbornly to her neck and temples, dark with sweat and steam, a chaotic halo around her head. Her usually smooth and composed hair now bristled with the urgency of a woman in command of far too many things at once. She moved like a small, efficient storm, issuing sharp, rapid-fire instructions to her children without pausing for breath, her hair swinging wildly with each swift turn and pivot. Phuong, looking like a nervous contestant on a cooking show, was meticulously setting the table, placing each utensil with the precision of an exam. Dung, meanwhile, was burning incense the wrong way, again, filling the air with acrid smoke. And Jackie, the youngest and most unpredictable, had just poured an entire rivulet of soy sauce across the only clean tablecloth, leaving a dark, spreading stain.

"That boy came way too early!" May muttered frantically, her voice a low growl of panic as she tried, with futility, to fix her eyeliner in the distorted reflection of a shiny pot lid. Her composure was cracking.

"No one's cleaned the bathroom yet!" she hissed, the horror dawning on her. At the threshold, Huy stood patiently, a picture of polite anticipation. In one hand, he held the pastel pink box of pastries from the local bakery, a peace offering, and in the other, a bouquet of slightly wilted, but earnestly presented, carnations. He bowed low, a deep, respectful gesture, his gaze deferential.

"Good evening, Auntie," he said, his voice earnest. "Thank you for giving me this opportunity to share a meal with your family."May, despite her inner turmoil, took a moment to look him up and down. His shirt was impeccably tucked in, and his shoes shone with a fresh polish. He had practiced this moment, this precise greeting, countless times in front of a mirror, striving for perfection.

"Come in, Huy. Don't stand there like a lamppost," she said, waving him in with a brisk, impatient hand, a hint of her usual bluntness cutting through her anxiety.

He stepped nervously into the warm, bustling apartment. He was immediately enveloped by a powerful symphony of smells: the familiar, pungent aroma of fish sauce, the sharp, clean scent of lemongrass, and something suspiciously, undeniably burning from the kitchen.

Chi, alerted by the doorbell and the sudden flurry of activity, came slowly, almost regally, down the stairs, pretending with an Oscar-worthy performance that she hadn't spent the last twenty minutes trying on every single pair of earrings she owned. She wore a simple, elegant dress, and for the first time in a while, she looked... genuinely shy, her usual confident demeanor softened by a rare vulnerability.

The family finally gathered around the beautifully laden table, a chaotic yet harmonious tableau. May had outdone herself, preparing a feast fit for royalty: steaming *canh chua* (Vietnamese sweet and sour soup), fragrant *cá kho tộ* (caramelized fish in a clay pot), a vibrant *gỏi gà* (chicken salad), and of course, a massive, fragrant pot of jasmine rice that could easily feed a small village.

Dinner started remarkably well, considering the earlier chaos. Huy was polite, attentive, and seemed to be making a good impression. Until, in a moment of eager politeness, he tried to scoop soup for May first, a traditional gesture of respect. His hand trembled slightly, and he accidentally spilled a generous ladle of the hot, savory liquid directly into her lap, leaving a large, dark stain on her clothes.

"Oh! I'm so sorry, Auntie! Oh no... I'm dead. I am so dead," Huy stammered, his face draining of all color, his eyes wide with genuine horror.

May froze, her spoon halfway to her mouth. The entire table froze. Phuong gasped audibly. Jackie whispered, her eyes huge, "He's dead. He's so dead." The air crackled with a palpable tension, a moment suspended between catastrophe and comedy.

But then, May let out a sudden, booming cackle, a rich, unexpected sound that filled the room. "Heavens, boy! Are you trying to make me any hotter than I already am? Are you trying to make me steam like my soup?" Her laughter was infectious, full-bodied, and utterly genuine.

The tension broke, dissolving instantly like sugar in hot tea. A wave of relieved laughter swept through the room, a joyous cacophony. Even Chi, who had been holding her breath, couldn't help but giggle as she quickly handed Huy a fresh napkin. "Good job, Huy," she whispered playfully, her eyes twinkling. "You're officially part of the chaos now. Welcome to the family.

Huy relaxed visibly after that, the rigid posture of his nervousness melting away. He engaged enthusiastically with Henry's questions about Vietnam, sharing poignant stories from the refugee camp, his voice warm with memory. He told anecdotes that captivated the younger children, who listened intently.

At the very end of the night, as Huy bowed politely, a gesture of profound gratitude, to take his leave, May stood by the door, arms crossed, studying him with a measured, knowing gaze. She saw more than just a polite young man; she saw a kind heart, a resilient spirit, and, more importantly, someone who might genuinely be right for her daughter, someone who could navigate the complexities of her family with grace and a good sense of humor.

Chi gave a small, contented sigh as she closed the door behind him, the sound barely audible. But later that night, as she sat on her bed, the quiet hum of the house surrounding her, she found herself turning one of Huy's folded paper cranes over and over in her hands, this one, she noticed, made from a vibrant, somewhat garish karaoke lyrics sheet. A soft, uncontrollable smile spread across her face, lingering, like someone who didn't want the sweetness of the night to end.

And May, sipping her tea quietly in the living room, a faint, contented smile playing on her lips, whispered to herself, "He only brought a few pastries, but somehow he fed the whole house with laughter and a warmth that truly fills the heart."

First Date (With 10,000 Aunties Watching)

The Tết Festival in Little Saigon was not just an event; it was a sensory explosion, a vibrant, sprawling celebration that consumed blocks of Westminster. Streets were joyfully closed to traffic, transforming into a pedestrian wonderland. Thousands of shimmering red lanterns, symbols of good fortune, swung gracefully from every lamppost, casting a warm, festive glow. The rhythmic, thunderous pounding of drums vibrated in the distance as magnificent lion dance teams warmed up, their colorful costumes poised for dazzling displays. The air was thick with an intoxicating symphony of aromas: the savory sizzle of grilled skewers, the sweet, earthy perfume of roasted chestnuts, and the delicate, spiritual scent of incense drifting from makeshift altars. It was undeniably beautiful, overwhelmingly loud, and utterly festive, a kaleidoscope of sound, sight, and smell. It was also, quite possibly, the absolute worst place on earth if you were trying to quietly, discreetly, go on your first date.

Chi, ever the master of self-deception, told herself it wasn't a date. "We're just going to see the lion dance," she insisted to her reflection, straightening the elegant lines of her traditional áo dài and applying just a tiny, barely perceptible hint of blush to her cheeks. "And maybe eat one thing. Maybe," she added, trying to sound nonchalant.

But as soon as she navigated the bustling crowd near the festival entrance and saw Huy waiting for her, a shy, hopeful smile on his face, holding a little red envelope specifically for her, her carefully constructed nonchalance crumbled. Her cheeks went warm, a blush deeper than any she had just applied.

"Chúc Mừng Năm Mới," he said, offering the envelope with a slight bow, his smile shy but genuine. "Happy New Year. For you. Lucky money. Even though you're not a kid anymore." His awkward English made her heart give a little flutter.

Chi took the envelope, pretending to roll her eyes with her usual playful sarcasm, but inside, a quiet thrill bloomed. "You're such a grandpa," she teased, though her voice was softer than she intended.

They began to stroll, swallowed by the festive current of the crowd. They paused to watch a calligraphy master, his brush moving with elegant precision, drawing out intricate, graceful characters for people's hopes and wishes: Phúc (happiness), Lộc (wealth), Thọ (long life). Huy, with a surprising boldness that made Chi's breath catch, then leaned in and quietly asked the master for one that said Tình Duyên, romance or destiny in love. Chi nearly choked on the sweet, translucent coconut jelly she had just bought, a blush spreading hotly across her entire face.

As they ate crispy bánh khọt (mini savory pancakes) from a bustling stall and sipped icy sugarcane juice, everything seemed to align perfectly, a rare moment of serene connection amidst the joyful chaos… until suddenly:

"CHI?! CON ĐANG LÀM GÌ Ở ĐÂY VỚI TRAI?!" (CHI?! WHAT ARE YOU DOING HERE WITH A BOY?!)

The voice, shrill and utterly unmistakable, belonged to Auntie Thu from the church. She seemed to materialize out of nowhere, appearing like a brightly colored ghost from the swirling crowd, holding a large bag of fragrant chả giò (fried spring rolls) and wearing a bright pink visor, a matching fanny pack, and the unmistakably outraged expression of someone who was about to report this scandalous sighting to every single other auntie in the entire church group, and beyond.

Then, as if summoned by an invisible, gossipy beacon, came Auntie Hằng. Then Uncle Bình, his brow furrowed with stern disapproval. Then, like a highly coordinated, well-oiled SWAT team of gossip, the entire Nguyễn family friend network began to converge, their eyes narrowed, their expressions a mixture of shock and avid curiosity.

Chi forced a tight, plastic smile onto her face, her cheeks burning. "We're just walking around!" she tried to explain, her voice a little too high, a little too strained.

Huy, caught completely off guard but instinctively reverting to ingrained cultural respect, bowed so many times, so low and rapidly, that he almost tipped over, barely catching himself. "Cháu chào các bác ạ. Cháu chỉ muốn làm bạn thôi," he stammered, trying desperately to explain. (Hello, aunties and uncles. I only want to be her friend.)

The aunties exchanged highly significant, knowing looks, their unspoken communication chillingly clear. One whispered loudly enough for Chi to hear, "Friend? Friend,

friend? A 'friend' who wears a freshly ironed white shirt and styles his hair with gel on a Sunday festival day?" The implication was crystal clear: no mere "friend" would exert such effort.

Eventually, after what felt like an endless, humiliating interrogation under the collective gaze of a thousand disapproving eyes, the aunties, satisfied they had extracted maximum information and delivered sufficient social pressure, finally moved on, melting back into the crowd like brightly plumed birds of prey. Chi and Huy stood frozen, the silence they left behind almost as deafening as their chatter.

"Remind me next time," Chi said, finally breaking the silence, her voice a low, dry murmur, "our second date should be in Antarctica. Or maybe the moon."

Huy laughed, a sound of pure, unadulterated relief. "Maybe Idaho. Fewer aunties."

They found a quiet bench near the edge of the festival and sank to rest, the cacophony of the celebration swirling around them. A vibrant lion dance team passed by, their drums shaking the very ground beneath their feet, and children squealing with delight. Huy leaned closer, his voice soft, thoughtful. "You embarrassed?"

Chi considered the question for a second, feeling the residue of the public scrutiny. Then, to her surprise, she shook her head. "No. You didn't run away when ten aunties attacked you like a pack of hungry wolves. That's pretty impressive, Huy."

He smiled, a genuine, shy curve of his lips. "Then I'm brave enough to ask one more thing."

She raised an eyebrow, a flicker of curiosity. "What?"

His gaze was direct, earnest. "Can I hold your hand?"

Chi looked around, her eyes sweeping the immediate vicinity, no aunties in sight, thankfully. She slowly, deliberately, offered her hand, her fingers trembling ever so slightly.

He took it gently, his touch warm and firm, his calloused palm a comforting presence against hers. And for a moment, in all the deafening noise and vibrant chaos of the Tết Festival, everything else faded away. Everything felt quiet, perfect, and utterly, wonderfully still.

From a nearby booth, where she was ostensibly admiring some floral arrangements, May watched the subtle, tender interaction with a cup of chè (sweet dessert soup) in her hand, pretending not to notice a single thing. But she couldn't help but whisper to herself, a soft, knowing smile

playing on her lips: "This New Year might bring romance...
but only if they survive the auntie patrol. And perhaps, only
if he buys better pants next time."

Mama's Love Story

It was late. The house had settled into a comfortable
silence, punctuated only by the distant hum of the
refrigerator. May sat at the dining table, bathed in the soft
glow of a single lamp, meticulously peeling transparent,
juicy longans into a small porcelain bowl, their sweet aroma
filling the air. Chi walked in, wearing her soft pajamas, her
long hair in a loose, comfortable braid, clearly unable to
sleep.

"Can't sleep?" May asked gently, not looking up
from her task, her voice calm and inviting.

Chi shrugged, a small, tired gesture. "Too many
thoughts in my head, Má."

May motioned for her to sit in the chair opposite her.
With practiced grace, she poured hot tea for both of them, its
steam rising in fragrant wisps, then slid the bowl of
glistening fruit over to Chi.

"I heard you and Huy talking in the backyard
earlier," May said softly, her voice quiet but direct,
confirming Chi's suspicion that very little escaped her
mother's notice. "You think you love him, con?"

211

Chi froze, caught off guard by the bluntness of the question. Her cheeks flushed in the dim light. "I... I don't know, Má. Maybe. Is that bad?" she whispered, feeling vulnerable.

May smiled, a small, tired, but infinitely knowing smile. "No, con. That's normal. That's how it starts."

There was a long, comfortable pause, filled only by the gentle clicking of May peeling fruit, before she spoke again, her voice a distant echo of memory.

"When I was your age, or even younger, I thought I knew what love was, too," she began, her gaze fixed on a distant point, lost in the past. "But back then, love didn't have time to wear makeup or go on pretty dates. It came like a storm... fast, loud, and full of fire. It came with the war."

Chi looked up, surprised, her teacup halfway to her lips. "You never told me about... him. My Ba." She realized then that she knew so little about her parents' true beginnings.

May's fingers paused on a longan, its delicate skin resisting her touch. She peeled it slowly, meticulously, her eyes distant, filled with the ghosts of memory. "He was much older than I and used to visit my aunt. He worked on boats with my cousin in Cà Mau, down in the Mekong Delta.

He was tall, quiet, and always smelled like the ocean and engine grease.

"The first time he looked at me, truly looked at me, I was carrying a whole tray of bánh bèo to market, and I dropped every single one." (Bánh bèo is a traditional Vietnamese dish, made from delicate rice flour and tapioca flour, often served with a savory topping.)

Chi grinned, picturing her usually composed mother in such disarray. "You? A mess?"

May nodded, a rare, soft chuckle escaping her lips. "I was a complete mess. But he didn't laugh. He helped me clean it all up, silently, without a single word of scorn. That's when I knew. That's when my heart truly settled."

She looked down at her tea, stirring it with a small spoon. "But we didn't have time, Chi. We never had enough time. The war came fast, like a relentless tide. And fear came even faster. Our village was no longer safe. We had to escape, to flee south, each day a gamble for survival. He told me he'd find a way… 'Don't be afraid, Little Lotus. I'll find you,' he promised."

Chi's voice softened, her eyes wide with the unfolding drama of her mother's past. "Did he? Did he find you?"

May's eyes shimmered, glistening with unshed tears as she stared out the window, truly lost in a powerful tide of memory. "The war broke everything, Chi. It shattered families and destroyed villages. We fled south with nothing but the clothes on our backs, just like so many others. I thought I'd lost him forever... that a love like ours, so young and fragile, couldn't possibly survive something so cruel, so devastating."

She paused, her voice wrapped in a delicate blend of profound sorrow and aching wonder, as she relived the impossible reunion. "But he never gave up. He never stopped searching. Through ruined roads, across treacherous rivers, through unimaginable danger and vast distances, he searched. Years passed, endless, desolate years, and then one day... he found me. He just walked into the little village where I was hiding, a small, dusty ghost of himself, like a dream I never dared to believe could come true."

She turned to Chi, her gaze steady, taking her daughter's hand with quiet, resolute strength. "It was him, Chi. It was your Ba. Your father. He found me. We married, quickly, quietly. And from the ashes of war, from nothing, we built a life, brick by painstaking brick. Ours was a true love story, the kind you read about in books, the kind that feels impossible, but rarer, infinitely more precious, when it's real."

May held Chi's gaze, her voice gentle but infused with an unshakeable certainty. "And I want you to remember this, always, my daughter: if it's real love, truly real, nothing can stop it. Not war, not time, not even fear. Real love finds a way."

May gently squeezed her hand, a transfer of strength. "Don't be sorry, con," she said softly, anticipating Chi's thoughts about her past sufferings. "That pain, those hardships, they taught me to be strong. They made me resilient. But it also showed me something important... Love isn't just grand gestures or pretty words. It's a sacrifice. It's about showing up, every single day, no matter what challenges come. It's commitment, even when it's hard."

She met her daughter's eyes, steady and unwavering, passing on a profound truth. "So, if you love him, Chi, don't be afraid. Stand by your feelings. Let your actions prove it, every single day. Just like your Ba proved his love to me."

Small Dinner (That Turned Into an Engagement Party)

Huy had meticulously crafted a plan, a deceptively simple one. He envisioned a quiet, intimate evening: he would invite May's family over for a small, casual dinner at

215

his uncle's house. Nothing fancy, just a cozy gathering. He'd wait for the perfect, serene moment, perhaps when the laughter softened or a quiet lull descended, then he would discreetly take out the ring and ask Chi the biggest, most life-altering question of his entire existence.

However, as Huy was rapidly learning, this was a Vietnamese family. And in the vibrant, sprawling, interconnected world of a Vietnamese family, even the most carefully laid plans do not, and cannot, survive the unstoppable forces of well-meaning uncles, overzealous aunts, or the lightning-fast spread of tin đồn (gossip).

By the time Chi arrived at his uncle's house, clutching her small handbag, she was greeted by a scene of glorious, joyful chaos. There were thirty-two, perhaps even forty, people packed into the living room, spilling out into the dining area, their voices a joyous cacophony. Someone had already roasted a whole, glistening pig, its crispy skin crackling, its savory aroma mingling with the other enticing scents. The karaoke machine, its colorful lights flashing, was already out and blaring, an uncle warming up with a heartfelt, slightly off-key rendition of "Con Đường Xưa Em Đi" (The Old Road You Traveled), a classic Vietnamese love song.

And, as if to underscore the delightful anarchy, two toddlers, fueled by sugar and boundless energy, were chasing each other wildly with a single, repurposed broomstick.

Chi leaned in close to Huy, her eyes wide with bewildered amusement. "Huy… what is all of this? What's going on?"

Huy, beads of sweat already forming on his brow despite the air conditioning, wiped them away with the back of his hand. "It was supposed to be just dinner, Chi, just a small, quiet dinner. I invited my uncle. He invited your mom. Your mom, in turn, invited the church ladies. And the church ladies, well, they invited their entire roster of cousins and distant relatives. One person even brought a wedding cake, a full three-tiered one! I don't even know who she is, I swear!" he whispered, his voice a blend of desperation and a burgeoning acceptance of the inevitable.

May, meanwhile, beaming radiantly in her best, impeccably embroidered áo dài, was already moving through the jubilant crowd like a general reviewing her troops, enthusiastically handing out plates of food. "Nó cầu hôn tối nay đó!" she declared proudly, her voice ringing out to a group of gasping aunties. (He's proposing tonight!)

The crowd erupted instantly in a joyous symphony of whispers, excited gasps, and thrilled squeals, a chorus of happy anticipation.

Chi's eyes snapped back to Huy, her mouth agape. "You haven't even asked me yet!" she hissed, a mixture of mortification and exasperation in her voice.

"I KNOW!" he whispered back, his voice strained, his grand, romantic plan dissolving into a hilarious spectacle.

Then, suddenly, dramatically, the lights in the living room dimmed, casting a soft, expectant glow. Someone, clearly an instigator, turned down the karaoke machine mid-sentence, cutting off the uncle's heartfelt ballad. A brave, perhaps slightly tipsy, uncle stepped forward, raising his glass and shouting, "Tới giờ rồi!" (It's time!)

Huy stood up, his heart pounding a frantic rhythm against his ribs. All thirty-two (or more) people, including the broomstick-wielding toddlers, turned their attention directly to him, dozens of phone cameras already raised, poised to capture the moment. He took a deep, shaky breath, walked towards Chi, and dropped to one knee, barely managing to dodge a determined toddler who chose that exact moment to crawl directly across his path.

He opened the small, velvet box, revealing the glittering ring, and looked up at Chi, his eyes full of love and a dash of bewildered humor. "Chi… I wanted to wait for the perfect moment for this," he began, his voice a little hoarse, "but I think we might have passed it about an hour ago." A wave of gentle laughter rippled through the expectant crowd.

"You make me braver," he continued, his voice gaining strength, "You make me better. You even get to choose the pants I buy, and that is a truly significant concession." More laughter erupted, even May giggling openly behind her teacup, a rare and delightful sound.

"So… will you marry me?" he finally asked, his gaze fixed solely on her.

Chi stared at him, then at the vast, expectant crowd holding back a collective scream of excitement, their faces alight with anticipation. She took a breath, a silent acknowledgment of the public spectacle.

"I was going to say yes privately," she declared, her voice carrying across the hushed room, a playful challenge in her eyes, "but since half of Westminster is watching…"

With a decisive move, she pulled him up from his knee, her hand finding his. "Yes," she whispered, her voice soft but firm, just for him.

The room exploded. Someone, anticipating the moment, lit a shower of handheld sparklers, showering the space with glittering gold. A distant cousin burst into tears of pure joy. An uncle, overcome with exuberance, began passing out bao lì xì (red envelopes filled with lucky money) "just for fun," ignoring the fact that it wasn't Tết anymore.

May stood back, her eyes a little teary, a lot proud, surveying the joyous chaos she had helped orchestrate. Then, with a voice that cut through the celebratory din, she shouted, "Okay! Everybody eats! We're Vietnamese, not fancy! There's enough food for everyone!"

That night, amidst the steaming bowls of fragrant bún bò Huế and the uninhibited chaos of karaoke, Chi and Huy became something more than a couple, they became a future. A future that was loud, fiercely loving, and vibrantly carrying the indomitable hope of a community that, after so much struggle and displacement, steadfastly refused to disappear, choosing instead to celebrate life, family, and new beginnings with every fiber of its being.

Chi and Huy's Wedding

Chi and Huy's wedding was never, under any circumstances, going to be a small affair. Not with two sprawling, interconnected families, three active church groups eager to celebrate, and a Vietnamese auntie network faster and more efficient than any morning news broadcast. After decades of war, displacement, and quiet suffering, these people were not just attending a wedding; they were ravenous for joy, for hope, for any tangible reason to believe in a beautiful, unblemished future. The entire community, a testament to resilience, was eager to witness and partake in this vibrant declaration of life.

The sacred ceremony itself took place in the very same church where Chi and Huy had first met, where the seeds of their connection had been quietly sown. Chi walked down the aisle, radiant and ethereal, wearing a stunning, deep red áo dài, its luxurious silk fabric intricately embroidered with majestic gold phoenixes, symbols of rebirth and good fortune. Her dark, lustrous hair was elegantly pinned up, adorned with fragrant jasmine blossoms, their delicate white petals contrasting beautifully with her rich attire. Every head in the packed church turned as she entered. Some spectators teared up, their eyes glistening with emotion, others whispered excitedly and playfully elbowed their neighbors, sharing in the palpable joy and anticipation.

Huy waited at the altar, a picture of nervous anticipation yet undeniable handsomeness, impeccably dressed in a sharp, tailored Western-style suit. Over his traditional white shirt, he wore a gleaming, intricately designed silk headpiece, a nod to his heritage that made him look somewhere between Vietnamese royalty and a very well-dressed, dignified bakery item. His palms were visibly sweating, a testament to the immense significance of the moment.

When Chi finally reached him at the altar, her eyes sparkling, she leaned in and whispered with a sly, knowing grin, "You look like a steamed bun, Huy. A very handsome steamed bun."

Huy didn't miss a beat, his nervousness momentarily forgotten. "You love it," he retorted, a playful twinkle in his eye.

They exchanged their formal vows in English, their voices straightforward and sincere. However, toward the emotional climax of the ceremony, they each recited a heartfelt, abbreviated version of their vows in Vietnamese, specifically for their beloved parents and the revered elders seated in the front rows. The words were simple, straightforward, and their accents, while softened by years in America, were still a little off, a charming blend of their past and present. But it didn't matter. What mattered was the profound way they looked at each other, their hands shaking slightly as they clasped, and their hearts, despite the nerves, beating steadily as one.

May sat in the very front row, her face serene, silent through most of the ceremony, her gaze fixed on her daughter. But when the officiant finally declared, his voice resonating through the church, "I now pronounce you husband and wife," she quietly reached up, wiped a single tear from the corner of her eye, and allowed a soft, profound smile to bloom across her face. Her mission was complete, her daughter's happiness secured.

The reception, a grand affair, was held at a large, bustling banquet hall, transformed into a magical wonderland. The ceiling was draped with twinkling fairy lights that glittered like a thousand tiny stars, and extravagant flower arrangements, a charming blend of cultures, suddenly included both delicate white roses and tall, graceful bamboo stalks. Some tables had elegant wine glasses, while others featured familiar soy sauce bottles, a testament to the diverse palates present. Every single guest's seat had a small, charming jar of homemade pickled vegetables as a party favor, May's idea, of course, a practical and heartfelt token of gratitude.

Chi changed into a flowing white gown for the celebratory party, but she kept her precious jade bracelet on, a treasured heirloom her mother had given her, which had been passed down through generations. The smooth green stone shimmered softly on her wrist as she gracefully raised a glass for the first toast, her new husband beaming beside her.

Dinner was a magnificent ten-course feast, a truly lavish spread that showcased the best of Vietnamese cuisine. There were succulent lobster noodles, glistening roast duck with crispy skin, perfectly fried shrimp, savory soups, and a towering, elaborate wedding cake, plus at least three additional types of traditional Vietnamese desserts to satisfy every sweet tooth. At one point, a small child cried dramatically because his spring roll unfortunately fell on the floor, and an uncle, without a single word of hesitation, immediately handed him his own, untouched spring roll, a gesture of quiet, communal generosity.

Toasts were given throughout the evening, some long-winded, some endearingly awkward, some profoundly touching, drawing tears and laughter in equal measure. One particularly jovial uncle ended his heartfelt speech by pointing directly at Huy and saying, his voice filled with a smile that was somehow both genuinely kind and subtly intimidating, "You take care of her now, young man. She is precious."

Then came the dancing. It started slow and romantic, Chi and Huy swaying gently to a classic ballad, their eyes locked in blissful adoration. But it quickly turned wild and exuberant when the DJ, sensing the shift in mood, unleashed the infectious energy of Bruno Mars. Chi danced freely and joyfully with her cousins, spinning and laughing. Huy, a little less naturally graceful, did his absolute best to keep up, his movements earnest and endearing. And even May, a rare sight, found herself on the dance floor, twirling with her sons, grinning like a carefree teenager the whole time, shedding years of worry in the embrace of happiness.

Later in the evening, as the festivities continued their joyful crescendo, May stepped outside for a moment, seeking a breath of fresh, cool air, her face flushed with warmth and contentment. A friend, noticing her slight fatigue, asked if she was tired.

"I'm tired," she said, sipping slowly from a refreshing glass of coconut water, a contented sigh escaping her lips, "but my daughter is happy. And that, my dear friend, that's all I ever wanted. All I ever truly dreamed of."

Meanwhile, Chi and Huy, seeking a moment of quiet intimacy amidst the joyous pandemonium, found a secluded corner away from the blaring music and dazzling lights. They sat side by side on a small bench, their shoes off, their feet aching from dancing, laughing softly, their shoulders touching.

"You ready for real life?" Huy asked, his voice soft, intimate.

Chi leaned her head against his shoulder, her heart full. "I've been ready since the day we met, Huy. Since the day you didn't run away from all those aunties."

From somewhere behind them, carried on the gentle breeze, May's voice, clear and resonant, rang out: "Don't forget to take home the leftovers! There's enough for a week!"

They both laughed, a shared, heartfelt sound of joy and acceptance. Their married life, loud, loving, and wonderfully messy, had officially begun.

A Humble Beginning in Anaheim

After the joyous, whirlwind celebration of their wedding, Chi and Huy embarked on their married life with hopeful hearts and skinny wallets. Their first home together was a humble single-room apartment in Westminster, a small, functional space that became their sanctuary amidst the bustling energy of Orange County. It wasn't much more than a combined living and sleeping area with a tiny kitchenette tucked into a corner, but it was theirs, a foundation for their new future.

Every morning, the scent of Chi's brewing Vietnamese coffee mingled with the faint, sweet smell of orange blossoms drifting in through their open window.

Money, or rather the distinct lack of it, was a constant, unspoken presence in their early days. Huy, ever the meticulous planner and provider, spent countless evenings hunched over a small, wobbly card table, poring over receipts, income statements, and real estate listings. He diligently crunched numbers, sketching out elaborate calculations on scraps of paper, trying to weigh the precarious balance of renting versus buying in the competitive Southern California market.

His background in law, though incomplete, had instilled in him a sharp analytical mind, and he could see that while their savings were meager, property ownership, even on a small scale, offered a path to long-term stability they desperately craved.

One evening, after weeks of careful deliberation, Huy looked up from his calculations, his eyes alight with a quiet determination. "Chi," he said, his voice firm, "we should buy. A condo. It will be tight, but it's a better investment.

Chi trusted him implicitly. She knew his dedication. Huy, a true embodiment of the immigrant work ethic, was already a relentless worker. His primary job was at a local auto repair shop, where he excelled with his sharp mind and tireless hands, often staying late into the evening.

But to make ends meet and save for his ambitious dream of homeownership, he frequently took on a second job, sometimes delivering pizzas late into the night, and other times working early morning shifts stocking shelves at a nearby grocery store. His days stretched long, often starting before dawn and ending well after midnight, fueled by strong Vietnamese coffee and an even stronger sense of responsibility.

He'd come home exhausted, his clothes smelling of oil, pizza, or cleaning supplies, but his spirit remained unbroken. Chi, in turn, supported him fiercely, managing their meager budget, cooking nourishing meals, and making their tiny apartment a haven of peace and comfort after his grueling shifts.

The Unexpected Offer from Disney

After months of relentless saving and diligent searching, Huy found it: a small, unassuming condominium unit in Anaheim. It was an older building, slightly worn around the edges, but the unit itself was bright, clean, and felt surprisingly spacious for its footprint. It had a modest living area, a compact kitchen that was still larger than their previous apartments, and a single bedroom that would perfectly fit their needs. It was within their reach, thanks to Huy's dual incomes and their disciplined savings. They stretched every penny, taking on a small, manageable mortgage, and officially became homeowners. Owning their piece of California, however small, felt like an immense victory, a tangible symbol of their hard work and perseverance.

They poured their limited energy into making it their own, painting the walls a cheerful cream, adding small, personal touches that transformed the stark space into a cozy home. The location, right on Harbor Boulevard close to Disneyland, was bustling, but they quickly grew accustomed to the constant flow of traffic and the distant, familiar hum of city life. What they didn't fully realize at the time was the actual strategic value of their new address.

Just a year later, a crisp, official-looking letter arrived in their mailbox, bearing the unmistakable, elegant Walt Disney Company logo. Chi opened it, her brow furrowed in confusion. Huy, having just returned from a long shift, peered over her shoulder as she read aloud, slowly at first, then with increasing disbelief.

The letter was a formal offer to purchase their condominium. Disney, in the midst of one of its ambitious expansion projects for the Disneyland Resort, was systematically acquiring properties to facilitate future developments, including parking structures and improved guest access. Their small condo, acquired through sheer grit and calculated risk, was now directly in the path of a multi-billion-dollar corporation's grand vision.

The offer was incredible. Disney was willing to pay three times what they had spent on the condo just twelve months earlier. It was an amount that, to Chi and Huy, seemed like they had hit the jackpot. Their initial investment, made out of necessity and hard work, was now about to produce an astonishing profit.

Chi looked at Huy, her eyes wide with disbelief and wonder. "Huy," she whispered, her voice barely audible, "three times... they're offering *three times* what we paid!"

Huy, usually stoic, felt a broad, uncharacteristic grin spread across his face. He shook his head, a mix of disbelief and immense relief washing over him. It was an offer they couldn't refuse, honestly. This unexpected windfall wasn't just money; it was a testament to their resilience, their courage, and Huy's shrewd foresight. It meant financial security they had only dreamed of, a springboard to a future far more comfortable than they had ever dared to imagine in that tiny single-room apartment. Their hard work had not just paid off; it had multiplied beyond their wildest dreams, all thanks to a little condo on Harbor Boulevard and a magical mouse.

A Strategic Leap: From Condo to Condos

The Disney offer was, in a word, transformative. Chi and Huy, still pinching themselves, promptly sold their humble condominium to the Disney Company, a transaction that was surprisingly swift and efficient, befitting a corporate giant. The three times their purchase price windfall landed in their bank account , a sum that felt utterly surreal, a dizzying mountain of money that dwarfed anything they had ever imagined possessing. This wasn't just profit; it was a Launchpad.

Huy, with his pragmatic mind and newfound financial leverage, immediately began to strategize. Their days of struggling paycheck to paycheck were over, but his vision stretched far beyond simple comfort. He saw an opportunity not for lavish spending, but for robust investment and long-term security. Although he may not have completed his university studies in Vietnam due to the war, his innate intelligence and the foundational legal training he received provided him with a sharp, analytical mind.

He diligently crunched numbers, sketching out elaborate calculations on scraps of paper, trying to weigh the precarious balance of renting versus buying in the competitive Southern California market. He meticulously researched, analyzing rental yields, property values, and the burgeoning demand fueled by the nearby theme parks and growing local population. He could see that while their savings were meager, property ownership, even on a small scale, offered a path to long-term stability they desperately craved.

His plan was bold: instead of buying a larger single home, they would leverage their substantial profit from the Disney sale to purchase multiple, smaller rental properties. The goal was to create a steady, passive income stream that would not only secure their financial future but also provide them with a degree of freedom and stability that their parents had never known.

Armed with their significant down payment, Chi and Huy, under Huy's diligent guidance, embarked on a whirlwind of property hunting. They focused their search on well-located, modest apartment units within Anaheim, units that were attractive to renters but didn't demand exorbitant prices. They poured over listings, attended open houses on their rare days off, and negotiated fiercely, drawing on Chi's charm and Huy's sharp analytical skills.

Within a few short months, they achieved what seemed impossible to their community: they successfully closed on three separate apartment units located in various strategic areas across Anaheim. These weren't grand, luxurious properties, but solid, well-maintained units in decent neighborhoods. The process was exhausting, a blur of paperwork, mortgage applications, and inspections, but with each set of keys they received, a profound sense of accomplishment settled over them.

The immediate profit from the Disney sale had been used as hefty down payments for these properties, significantly reducing their mortgage burdens and making the ventures feasible. The remaining cash, carefully budgeted, covered immediate repair needs and initial vacancy periods. This strategic move meant their financial destiny was no longer tied to a single job or a single property. They had diversified, building a small but formidable real estate portfolio.

This period marked a pivotal shift for Chi and Huy. The sheer scale of the undertaking meant Huy continued to work tirelessly, though perhaps with a different kind of drive now. He kept his job at the auto repair shop, but his evenings and weekends were now devoted to managing their burgeoning rental properties. He'd wake up early to drive to one of their units, fixing a leaky faucet, repairing a creaking door, or painting a wall himself, rather than hiring costly contractors.

His hands, already accustomed to the grease of auto mechanics, now expertly handled plumbing and carpentry. In the evening, after a full day of manual labor, instead of resting, he would sit down at their small dining table, poring over spreadsheets, calculating how to invest their next rental income, manage property expenses, and strategically pay down mortgages. Chi, meanwhile, took on the administrative side, meticulously tracking finances, drafting leases, and fostering good relationships with their new tenants.

Their modest single-room apartment life was now a distant memory, replaced by the exhilarating, exhausting reality of being property owners. The Disney offer hadn't just bought them a new beginning; it had propelled them into an entirely new chapter of entrepreneurship and financial independence, a testament to their unwavering work ethic and wise decisions.

A Sacred Announcement: A New Life for the Trần Family

The subtle changes had been evident for weeks, though only May, with her keen maternal instincts and a lifetime of observing women, seemed to notice them. Chi, usually so vibrant and energetic, had a new softness about her, a gentle flush to her cheeks that wasn't just from the California sun. Her appetite, typically robust, swung wildly, sometimes craving the tartness of green mangoes, other times recoiling from the smell of jasmine rice. One crisp morning, as May prepared a light breakfast, she caught Chi's gaze across the kitchen. A silent, knowing understanding passed between them, a warmth blooming in May's chest. Chi's occasional bouts of morning sickness, discreetly managed, had not escaped her mother's vigilant eye either.

Later that afternoon, after Huy had left for the auto shop and the rental calls had quieted, Chi sat down with her mother. Her hands trembled slightly as she spoke, confirming what May already suspected. A visit to the doctor, a discreet appointment made weeks ago, had confirmed the joyous news. For a moment, silence hung in the air, broken only by the distant hum of traffic on Harbor Boulevard. Then, with a soft, choked gasp, May's eyes welled with tears of profound joy. She didn't shout or leap up; instead, she reached across the table, her hands gently enveloping Chi's. "Con gái, con gái của Má," she whispered, her voice thick with emotion, her touch light as a feather. "My daughter, my dear daughter."

Tears streamed down May's face, not of sorrow, but of an overwhelming, ancient happiness. She held Chi's hands tightly, her gaze fixed on her daughter's glowing face. "Thank you," she murmured, a deep, heartfelt whisper. "Thank you to Heaven and our blessings for the continuation of our family." It was a moment steeped in centuries of tradition, a recognition of life's sacred cycle through a lens of faith.

The news, once confirmed, didn't spread with boisterous fanfare, but rather with the soft, tender reverence characteristic of their close-knit Vietnamese family. The first to know, after May, was, of course, Huy. When Chi told him later that evening, his exhaustion from a double shift melted away, replaced by an expression of awe and disbelief. He held her close, murmuring blessings and promises, his hands gently tracing circles on her still-flat stomach.

The next morning, May began her own quiet, traditional celebration. She rose even earlier than usual, her movements infused with a new, joyful purpose. She meticulously gathered the ingredients for chè bà bầu, a sweet and nourishing soup traditionally prepared for pregnant women. The kitchen filled with the comforting aroma of lotus seeds, red dates, and longans simmering gently, a fragrant testament to her love and care. She prepared a large bowl for Chi, urging her to eat every spoonful for strength and health, emphasizing the belief that nourishing the mother would also nourish the baby.

That evening, the entire family gathered, not for a party, but for a solemn and beautiful moment of shared faith. May brought out her rosary beads, smooth and worn from years of prayer. Together, the family knelt in the living room before a cherished statue of the Virgin Mary, their heads bowed in quiet devotion. They prayed together, their voices soft, asking God for His grace and blessings upon Chi's pregnancy, for a smooth journey, and a healthy, fortunate child. It was a tangible connection to their faith, a plea for divine blessings for their future, echoing the profound gratitude felt by generations before them.

The official, more public, but still intimately family-centric announcements began soon after. There were no flashy "gender reveal" parties. Instead, subtle, joyous hints were dropped within their community and church circles. May would casually mention to a fellow parishioner, "Chi's looking very well these days, very... blessed." Huy's uncle, a devout Catholic himself, would offer a knowing wink and a new, more expensive bao lì xì to Chi "for good luck and God's favor."

Then, a more intimate form of announcement began to circulate. A new, lovingly knitted baby blanket was discreetly placed on the sofa when visitors came, or a small, intricately folded paper crane, like the ones Huy used to make her, next to a tiny pair of baby booties placed on the mantelpiece. The news spread like wildfire through their extensive network, not through impersonal broadcasts, but through excited phone calls, whispered congratulations at the market, and knowing smiles exchanged across church pews. Soon, the news reached every corner of their community, heralded by word of mouth more than any formal announcement: "Coming soon: Baby Trần!" The family line, forged through war and displacement, was not just continuing; it was flourishing, blossoming anew in the

238

vibrant soil of their American home, watched over by their faith and the love of their family.

A Crossroads: Minh's Difficult News

Life in the May household had settled into a comforting rhythm during Chi's pregnancy, each day brought new signs of anticipation and growth. Chi's belly rounded a little more, a beautiful, visible testament to the new life flourishing within her. Her morning sickness faded, replaced by a steady, healthy appetite and a serene glow. The children, too, were thriving. Hoang, still diligently juggling school and work, had found his footing in high school, his grades steadily improving. Long and Duy, though still prone to their adventurous escapades, excelled in their studies, their boundless energy channeled into newfound academic curiosity.

Sang, always the responsible one, continued to be a pillar of support, helping May with chores and looking after her younger siblings. The rental properties were generating a stable income, and Huy's dual roles as mechanic and landlord kept him busy but fulfilled. Everything seemed to be moving in the right direction, a harmonious blend of progress and anticipation.

Then, one quiet Tuesday evening, as the family gathered for dinner, a familiar tension settled over the table.

Minh, usually so jovial and talkative, was unusually subdued. He picked at his food, his gaze distant, his brow furrowed. May, ever sensitive to the moods of her children, noticed immediately. "Minh, con," she began softly, using the affectionate term for her son, "is something wrong? You're quiet tonight."

Minh hesitated, setting down his chopsticks. He looked at his mother, then at his siblings, his gaze lingering on Chi's swelling belly. He had rehearsed this conversation countless times in his head, trying to find the words that wouldn't cause pain or disrupt the delicate balance of their newfound happiness. He knew he had to decide, and he had to talk about it now.

"Má," he started, his voice a little strained, "I… I received a job offer today."

A ripple of quiet excitement went through the younger kids. A job offer was good news, always. But May's eyes, fixed on Minh, saw the underlying struggle.

"That's wonderful, con," she said, cautiously optimistic. "What kind of job?"

Minh took a deep breath. "It's… It's a manager position, Má. With a big company. Excellent pay, more than

I could make here for a long time." He paused, the hard part catching in his throat. "But... I have to move to Texas."

The words hung in the air, heavy and unexpected. Texas. It wasn't just another city; it was a distant state, a world away from their tightly woven community in Orange County. The laughter and chatter around the table died instantly. Chi's hand instinctively went to her stomach.

Minh continued, his voice softer, trying to explain the gravity of the opportunity. "It's a one-time opportunity, Má, a chance to step into management, to grow my career. The pay is excellent, enough to truly help us all, more than I can imagine right now. My manager here even said it's a perfect fit for me, a chance I might not get again." He looked earnestly at May, seeking her understanding, her blessing. He knew this would be hard, but the logical part of his mind, the part that had absorbed years of their family's struggle, screamed that he couldn't let this go. It was a chance for him to contribute truly, to live up to the unspoken expectations of providing for his family, just as his parents had always done.

May's face remained impassive, but her eyes held a flicker of deep sadness, though she quickly masked it. Her oldest son, her rock, her first child born in Vietnam, was considering leaving the nest they had so painstakingly built together. The thought was a sharp pang. This was the first true fissure in their close-knit unit since they'd landed in America. She understood the lure of opportunity, the immigrant drive for betterment, but the thought of Minh, so far away, felt like a piece of her heart preparing to detach. The room remained silent, everyone waiting for May's response, the unspoken question hanging heavy in the air: how would their matriarch react to this difficult choice?

Minh's words hung in the air, a silent bomb ticking in the small, crowded living room. The younger children, initially buoyant with the prospect of "good news," sensed the shift in atmosphere and quieted, their innocent faces mirroring the sudden tension. May's earlier cautious optimism evaporated, replaced by a familiar ache she'd carried for years – the relentless push and pull of opportunity and separation.

She looked at Minh, the one who'd shouldered so much since they arrived in California. He was a man now, his lean frame still holding the echo of the lanky boy who'd arrived in this new country, wide-eyed and terrified. He had worked tirelessly, taken every odd job, his hands calloused, his spirit unyielding. He'd learned English faster than any of them, navigating the bewildering new systems, always putting his family first. Now, this.

"Texas," she repeated, the word foreign and distant on her tongue. It sounded like another world, far beyond their familiar, bustling neighborhood.

Minh nodded, his gaze fixed on a point just beyond her shoulder, unable to meet her eyes. "It's for Special Project Assignment, Má. A Project Manager position. They specialize in developing new software and technology. It's a huge step up. Benefits: a real career path. It's everything I've been working towards."

He finally looked at her, his dark eyes pleading for understanding. "I know it's far. I know it's not what we planned. But Má, this is… this is a chance, a chance to help us. To ensure the family's security and to pay for the kids' school education, so they don't have to struggle like we did. Maybe even… maybe even bring you out there one day, when I'm settled."

The words tumbled out, a torrent of hope and desperation. May listened, her heart a tangled knot of pride and dread. She saw the longing in his eyes, the yearning for something more, something he deserved after years of sacrifice. But she also saw the looming void his absence would create. Who would help with the younger ones? Who would be her rock, her translator, her protector in this sometimes-confusing land?

A gust of wind rattled the single-paned window, and for a moment, May was transported back to another time, another difficult decision, another wrenching separation. She remembered the fear, the uncertainty, but also the fierce determination that had propelled them forward.

She reached out, her calloused hand finding Minh's arm, squeezing it gently. "Texas is a long way, con. A very long way." Her voice was soft, laced with an unspoken question: Are you sure you're ready to leave us? Are you sure we're prepared for you to go?

May's Difficult Decision

The silence that followed Minh's announcement stretched, taut and heavy, broken only by the distant hum of the refrigerator. Each second felt like a minute, each minute an hour. The younger children instinctively looked at May, sensing the immense weight of the moment, the shift in the family's carefully constructed stability. Chi's hand rested protectively on her growing belly, her gaze fixed on her mother, whose face remained a mask, revealing nothing of the tumultuous emotions surely raging within.

May's mind raced, a whirlwind of memories and calculations. She thought of their perilous escape from

244

Vietnam, the agonizing choices she had made to keep her children safe, whole, and together. She remembered the gnawing hunger, the freezing nights in Idaho, the endless hours she had spent folding laundry and boxes, her hands aching, all to build this new life, this sense of belonging, this family unit. They had endured so much, always together, always relying on each other. Minh, her firstborn, the quiet protector, had been a constant presence, a steady anchor in every storm.

To send him away, to willingly fragment their painstakingly reunited family, felt like tearing a piece of her flesh. Her heart screamed to forbid it, to cling to the warmth of his presence, especially now, with Chi's pregnancy bringing such new joy and vulnerability. The very thought of him alone in a distant state, without his family's daily comfort and support, twisted her gut. It was a primal fear, born of displacement and loss.

But then, the other voice, the one forged in the crucible of survival, asserted itself. It was the voice of the shrewd market vendor, the resourceful mother, the immigrant who understood that opportunity, when it knocked, often did so only once. She looked at Minh, her strong, intelligent son, his shoulders now slumped with the unspoken burden of his ambition.

She saw the longing in his eyes, the deep desire to prove himself, to secure a future far beyond the one they currently inhabited. This wasn't just a job for him; it was a ladder, a chance for upward mobility, a step into a professional world that had been denied to her generation. It was the very reason they had endured everything to come to this country.

Her children's success was her success, their dreams her dreams. If she held him back, out of her fear or need, she would be stifling the very potential they had risked everything to unlock. It would be an act of selfishness, a betrayal of the sacrifices they all had made. She knew that true love and true familial support sometimes demanded the hardest renunciations.

Finally, May straightened her shoulders, drawing a deep, almost imperceptible breath. Her voice, when it came, was low, firm, and surprisingly devoid of overt emotion, a testament to her iron will. "Minh," she began, her eyes holding his, "this opportunity... it is a good one, for you. For your future." She paused, letting the words sink in, emphasizing the individual nature of his path. "You have always been responsible. You have always worked hard. You have earned this."

Her gaze swept over each of her children, resting for a moment on Chi's concerned face. "We came here to build a new life, for all of us. And building means sometimes we must take risks. It means we must let our birds fly, even when the nest feels empty without them." Her eyes softened for a brief instant, betraying the immense effort this decision cost her. "Go, Minh. Take this job. Make it a success."

But her voice hardened slightly, a subtle warning woven into her blessing. "But you remember who you are. You remember your family. You call your Má every week. You visit when you can. And you always, always look out for your siblings, no matter the distance. This family," she declared, her hand sweeping to encompass them all, "is your foundation. Don't you ever forget that, even in Texas."

It was a decision born of incredible fortitude – hard, breaking in its emotional toll, yet profoundly smart in its strategic vision for Minh's future and, by extension, the collective prosperity of the family. May had chosen not to preserve the present merely, but to invest in a potentially brighter future, even if it meant a temporary, painful separation. The silence at the table shifted then, from tension to a respectful awe for their mother's unwavering strength and foresight.

The Arrival of Charlotte: Huy's Unforgettable Night

The call came in the dead of night, jarring Huy awake with a frantic urgency. It was the landline, a shrill ring that sliced through the quiet Anaheim night. "Huy! It's time! I think it's time!" Chi's voice, usually calm and composed, was laced with a mix of pain and excitement. Huy, who had spent months meticulously preparing for this moment by reading every pregnancy book Chi brought home and even timing her Braxton Hicks contractions (much to her annoyance), found all his carefully acquired knowledge dissolving into a flurry of panicked movements.

He stumbled out of bed, fumbling for his car keys, his wallet, anything essential. His carefully packed hospital bag, which he had organized with military precision weeks ago, suddenly felt alien in his trembling hands. "Okay! Okay, Chi, breathe! Just like we practiced! Small breaths, like a bird eating rice!" he blurted, his breathing ragged.

Getting Chi into the car was an adventure in itself. She was surprisingly agile for someone in labor, but Huy, convinced she might spontaneously combust, hovered nervously, opening doors, offering a hand, and almost tripping her twice in his eagerness. The drive to the hospital, usually a familiar fifteen minutes down the dimly lit streets, stretched into an eternity. Every bump in the road felt like a mountainous tremor. "Is that a contraction? Are you sure that's not a contraction? We're almost there, I promise!" he chanted, gripping the steering wheel so tightly his knuckles were white.

They arrived at the hospital in a breathless rush. Huy, trying to maintain an air of dignified composure, managed to tell the admissions desk, "My wife is... birthing! A baby! Right now, I think!" The nurses, well-accustomed to frantic new fathers, efficiently whisked Chi away.

And then, Huy was left alone in the waiting room, the silence deafening after the chaos. He tried to sit, but instantly sprang back up. He paced, he stopped, he stared at the clock, its hands moving with agonizing slowness. He tried to read a magazine, but the words swam before his eyes. The wait was unbearable. Every distant cry from the nursery, every whispered conversation from the nurses' station, sent a jolt of adrenaline through him. He was ready to be a dad, he truly was, but the sheer power of the unknown, the vulnerable anticipation, was overwhelming.

Just as he was contemplating whether he should offer to fix a flickering light fixture in the hallway (a habit from his landlord duties), the doors to the waiting room swung open. May and Hoang walked in, their faces etched with palpable anxiety, having driven over as soon as they received Huy's frantic call from the hospital lobby. May, ever the stoic, clutched her worn rosary beads, her lips moving silently in prayer. Hoang, looking more like a worried young man than a confident high schooler, paced even faster than Huy, his brow furrowed.

"Any news, Huy? Is she okay? Is the baby okay?" May asked, her voice a hushed urgency.

Huy shook his head, running a hand through his already disheveled hair. "They just took her. I don't know anything yet, Má. It's... It's a long wait."

The three of them then settled into a nervous vigil. May sat quietly, her prayers a constant murmur. Hoang fidgeted, checking his watch every thirty seconds. And Huy, in a desperate attempt to feel useful, began to silently calculate the square footage of the waiting room, wondering if it was a good investment for a future rental property, anything to distract from the agonizing wait.

Hours crawled by. The night deepened, the hospital growing quieter save for the occasional distant beep or muffled voice. May offered Huy sips of lukewarm tea from her thermos, a gesture of comfort. Hoang tried to engage him in a discussion about car engines, a clumsy attempt to distract them both. Each passing minute tightened the knot of anticipation in Huy's chest. He thought of Chi, enduring everything, and a profound wave of love and gratitude washed over him, mixed with a healthy dose of pure, unadulterated terror.

Finally, just as the first hints of dawn began to paint the sky outside the waiting room window, a nurse with a warm smile appeared. "Mr. Huy?" she said softly. "You have a beautiful baby girl. And Mrs. Chi is doing wonderfully."

Huy's knees almost buckled. He looked at May, whose face instantly broke into a radiant, tearful smile. Hoang let out a whoop of relief. "A girl!" Huy whispered, the words catching in his throat.

In that moment, all the calculations, all the nervous pacing, all the hours of waiting faded away. His new daughter had arrived, and the world had just become a much more wonderful, and wonderfully terrifying, place.

He saw Chi first, exhausted but radiant, her eyes already fixed on the small, swaddled form the nurse was gently tending to. When his gaze fell upon his daughter, a breath he didn't know he was holding escaped him. She was so small, so perfect.

A moment later, the nurse laid her in Chi's arms. Huy drew closer, his hand trembling slightly as he reached out to touch a tiny, clenched fist.

"Hello," he whispered, his voice thick with emotion.

Chi looked up at him, her smile weary but full of profound peace. "Huy," she said softly. "She's the answer to our prayers."

He nodded, unable to speak as he traced the delicate curve of his daughter's cheek. Memories of the past months rushed through him, the nights of uncertainty, the frightening doctor's visit in the second trimester, the long, quiet hours they had spent in their church's adoration chapel. He remembered the prayer they had whispered together, a shared secret in the stillness of the night.

It was Chi who chose the name **Charlotte** because it means "free person", a quiet tribute to the freedom they had risked everything. , dignified, resilient, and unbound. It was more than a name; it was a hope for a life no longer chained by war or fear. "Charlotte," Chi murmured, her voice barely audible. "Our little Charlotte."

The name landed in Huy's heart with the weight of a sacrament. It wasn't just a name they'd picked from a book; it felt as though it had been given to them. "Charlotte" meant "small" and "humble," a perfect reflection of their tiny daughter who had already brought them to their knees. But it also carried the immense strength and unwavering faith they had prayed for. In their own lives, they had walked their road to Damascus, and in an instant, their world had been turned upside down and filled with a blinding, beautiful light. Their daughter embodied that transformation.

They soon met their precious Charlotte, a tiny bundle who immediately captured all their hearts. Huy looked at her, then back at Chi, a wave of protectiveness and overwhelming love washing over him. He was a dad now, and though he had no idea what he was doing, he knew he was ready to learn.

Đầy Tháng: Charlotte's Grand Introduction

The first month of Charlotte's life was a sacred, secluded bubble for Chi and Huy. Following Vietnamese tradition, Chi and the newborn primarily stayed at home, observing a period of "lying-in" dedicated to rest and recovery for Chi, as well as to protect Charlotte from the outside world and potential illnesses. While Chi chafed slightly at the confinement, she understood its purpose and came to appreciate the quiet intimacy of those early weeks. Huy, ever the vigilant protector, made sure they had everything they needed, managing the rental properties and his job with renewed focus. Each evening, he returned home to the profound miracle of his daughter.

As Charlotte approached her one-month birthday, the Đầy Tháng (First Full Month Celebration), the quiet solitude began to shift into excited anticipation. This was to be Charlotte's official introduction, not just a casual family gathering, but a profoundly significant event where she would be formally presented to the extended family, close friends, neighbors, and their tight-knit Vietnamese community. It was the most essential early tradition, a joyous proclamation of new life and the continuation of their lineage.

May, now released from her self-imposed restraint of hovering constantly, bustled with energy, overseeing every detail of the celebration to be held at her house. The day began with a small, solemn ceremony to thank the Mười Hai Bà Mụ (12 Midwife Goddesses). Though Catholic, the family respectfully honored this ancient belief, seeing it as an expression of gratitude for the safe passage of mother and child. Before a small, beautifully arranged table, simple offerings were laid out: fresh flowers, carefully cooked rice, steaming cups of fragrant tea, artfully prepared sticky rice, and an array of traditional sweet desserts, such as chè. May gently held Charlotte, murmuring soft words of thanks to the unseen goddesses, asking for their continued protection and for Charlotte to be blessed with good fortune, intelligence, and beauty. Chi and Huy stood beside her, bowing their heads in quiet reverence.

Soon after, guests began to arrive, filling May's house with laughter, chatter, and the rich scents of festive food. Each arrival brought a chorus of "Cháu dễ thương quá!" (The baby is so cute!) as they converged to catch a glimpse of the guest of honor. Guests brought gifts, a steady stream of blessings for Charlotte. There were shimmering gold earrings, delicate and miniature, intended to adorn her ears as she grew. Piles of soft, vibrant baby clothes accumulated quickly. Many hands pressed money into Chi's palm or offered symbolic red envelopes (lì xì), their crisp paper promising good luck and prosperity. Every gift was received with heartfelt thanks, a tangible expression of the community's joy and support.

Amidst the joyful chaos, a special moment arrived. Though Charlotte had been given her English name at birth, this was the day her parents would officially announce her Vietnamese name, chosen with great care. Huy, holding Charlotte tenderly, stood beside Chi. "Today," he announced, his voice filled with pride, "we formally introduce our daughter. Her name is Trần Hương Lan." The name, meaning "Fragrant Orchid," was met with murmurs of approval and admiration, a beautiful blend of grace and resilience, perfectly suited for their new blossom.

The Đầy Tháng celebration was more than just a party; it was a profound affirmation of life, family, and community. It was a bridge between their ancient traditions and their new American reality, all woven together by the overwhelming love for little Charlotte. Charlotte was May's first and only grandchild, a tiny beacon of the family's thriving future. This new addition deeply affected May's children, as well as Charlotte's aunts and uncles, who felt a profound pull of new kinship.

Ngoc, the youngest of May's children and Charlotte's aunt, was utterly captivated. A quiet awe replaced her usual boisterous energy as she gazed at the tiny baby, reaching out a hesitant finger to touch Charlotte's cheek. She whispered secret stories to her, promising to teach her how to play hide-and-seek when she was older. Trong, Charlotte's uncle and a few years older, found himself drawn into the orbit of the new arrival, feeling an unexpected swell of protective affection. He offered to push Charlotte's stroller, a rare act of volunteerism, and found himself smiling at her tiny yawns.

Sang, Charlotte's aunt and always the curious one, peppered Chi and Huy with questions about babies, fascinated by every detail of this new life. She felt a surge of pride knowing this tiny person was part of her immediate family, a feeling of legacy she hadn't anticipated. Long, Charlotte's uncle, entertained Charlotte with silly faces, his usual mischief replaced by a desire to elicit a smile or gurgle from the baby. And then there was Duy, May's gifted son and Charlotte's beloved uncle. His connection to Charlotte was perhaps the most tender, an emotional bridge built on quiet observation and deep affection. He'd sit beside Charlotte's bassinet, his gaze soft, a silent promise in his eyes to always look out for his new niece, solidifying his role as "Uncle Duy."

At one point, May, noticing Duy's devoted gaze, gently took a tiny piece of sticky rice from an offering plate and, with a knowing wink, pretended to dab it on Charlotte's forehead, then playfully touched it to Duy's lips. "So you will always be sweet to her, like this sticky rice, con," she murmured, drawing laughter and a shy, pleased smile from Duy, a special blessing for his unique bond with the baby.

They all felt it, a deep, almost primal joy at the expansion of their direct family, a renewed sense of purpose in cherishing this new life and carrying forward their shared heritage.

The Hard Farewell: Minh's Departure

The weeks following Charlotte's Đầy Tháng were a bittersweet countdown to Minh's departure. The joyful echoes of the celebrations still lingered in May's house, but beneath that warmth, a quiet sadness settled in. Minh, usually stoic and self-contained, began to linger just a little longer after meals. His eyes often rested on his younger siblings, and every now and then, he would glance over at Charlotte, peacefully sleeping in her bassinet. His plane ticket had been purchased, and his modest belongings were packed. Now, the day of departure had arrived.

The entire family gathered at May's house, not for a party, but for a solemn farewell. The air hummed with unspoken emotions. There were no loud goodbyes or grand speeches, only the heavy quiet of a son preparing to leave the nest for the first time, venturing into the unknown world of a new state. May moved around the house, her actions precise, almost mechanical, as she prepared a simple meal. But her eyes, betraying the tremor in her heart, constantly sought out Minh, trying to commit every angle of his face, every familiar gesture to memory.

Before he left for the airport, Minh found May in the kitchen, her back to him as she stirred a pot of soup. He took a deep breath, his words heavy on his tongue.

"Má," he began, his voice thick with emotion, "I... I want to thank you. For everything. For bringing us here to America." He paused, swallowing hard. "I know it was so hard. You risked everything. You gave us this chance, this life. This job, this opportunity... it's all because of what you did." He reached out, gently taking her hand, his palm rough from years of hard work. "Thank you for letting me go, Má. For understanding."

May turned slowly, her hand trembling slightly in his. Her eyes, usually so strong, were glistening with unshed tears. For a moment, she just looked at him, her eldest son, the one who had carried so much unspoken responsibility on his young shoulders, even as a boy in Vietnam. The one who had faced unimaginable hardship, yet still emerged with ambition and integrity.

Then, a small, profound smile touched her lips, a smile of immense pride that briefly eclipsed her sorrow. "Minh, con," she said, her voice soft but firm, carrying a weight of deep conviction that resonated through the quiet kitchen. "Don't ever thank me for bringing us here." She squeezed his hand, her grip surprisingly strong. "You are the hero, Minh. Without you, we couldn't have made it. You saved this family."

Minh's brow furrowed in protest, ready to argue, to credit her strength, her courage.

But May shook her head, cutting him off gently. Her gaze remained unwavering. "No, con. Do you remember those first years? When did we have nothing? It was you. You were still a boy, but you worked beside me. You helped me understand this new world. You were strong when I was tired. You protected your younger siblings. You worked every job, saved every penny, helped us buy our first apartment, and helped us manage the rentals. You bore burdens no child should bear. You kept this family together, Minh." A single tear finally escaped, tracing a path down her cheek. "You saved the family, Minh. You are our hero. Now go, make your own life. Make us proud. Just remember, your family is always here, always waiting for you to come home."

The raw honesty of her words, the depth of her gratitude, shattered something in Minh. He leaned forward, embracing his mother tightly, his own eyes welling up. It was a hug that conveyed years of unspoken understanding, of shared struggles, and an unbreakable love. He was leaving, but he wasn't leaving behind the heart of his family. He was carrying it with him, this legacy of resilience and love, shaped by his mother.

With a final squeeze, he picked up his bag, cast one last look around the familiar kitchen, and walked out the door, ready to face his future, fortified by his mother's unwavering belief in him.

A Distant Echo from Vietnam

Over ten long, agonizing years, he had endured captivity, snatched by the North Vietnamese forces and wrenched far from the life he once knew, from his beloved family, from everything familiar. The re-education camp had stripped him bare, forcing him to endure soul-crushing monotony, relentless interrogations, gnawing hunger, and backbreaking labor under the indifferent gaze of his captors. Each day was a battle for survival, sustained only by the faint, flickering hope of reunion.

When he was finally released from the "re-education camps," a ghost of his former self, his first instinctive thought was home. He boarded a cramped, dilapidated bus to Saigon, a city teeming with unfamiliar faces and jarring reminders of the war's aftermath. From there, desperate to cover ground, he pieced together his journey south, hitching rides on rumbling trucks, enduring the dusty, jostling discomfort for hours on end. But for the last 20 miles to Vĩnh Long, the very thought of waiting for another bus was unbearable. The pull of home, the visceral need to see his family, tugged at his chest like a rope drawn impossibly tight, leaving him breathless. He couldn't bear to wait.

Every single step of that final leg was driven by an overwhelming longing, by years of suffocating silence and crushing absence, by phantom dreams of voices he hadn't heard in so long they echoed like ghosts in his memory. He walked through the night, his aching feet forgotten, because the desperate need to see them-to see home, to confirm they were real, was louder than any physical pain, louder than any logical reason.

And then, finally, as the first pale light of dawn began to soften the edges of the world, he stood in front of the house. His heart pounded like it might tear through his ribs, a frantic drum against his thin frame. It was his home, unmistakably, yet everything about it looked and felt profoundly unfamiliar, like a cherished memory distorted by time, wrapped in a suffocating fog. The windows were different, perhaps replaced. The garden, once meticulously tended, was wildly overgrown, choked with weeds. But the distinct scent of the humid air, heavy with the perfume of the

Mekong Delta, the familiar tilt of the roof, the curve of the ancient mango tree in the yard, those were unequivocally the same.

He hesitated, breath caught in his throat, unsure if this moment was truly real or just another cruel, exquisitely detailed dream, one of the many that had tormented him in the dark silence of his confinement and so many times he had imagined this reunion, clung to the hope of it like a fragile lifeline. Now, with the doorsteps away, it felt almost impossible to believe. He was different. Profoundly, irrevocably different.

His clothes, borrowed and ill-fitting, hung loosely on his skeletal frame. Years in the re-education camp had stripped him down to skin and bone, leaving him gaunt, almost translucent. His face was a map of suffering, weathered by the relentless sun, etched with lines born of silence and hardship. His eyes, once bright with laughter, sparkling with life, were now hollow, sunken deep in their sockets, searching desperately for something that might never return, a lost piece of himself. His hands trembled uncontrollably, not just from sheer exhaustion, but from the cumulative effect of years of chronic hunger, brutal forced labor, and soul-crushing isolation.

The man who had once filled this yard with vibrant stories, boisterous laughter, and heartfelt songs now stood like a spectral ghost outside his own home, a stranger to himself.

The wooden gate creaked mournfully as he pushed it open, the sound echoing in the pre-dawn stillness. The small yard was indeed a tangle of overgrown weeds and wild grasses. The old swing, where his children used to play, swayed gently in the nascent breeze, as if remembering them, a poignant, silent accusation of his long absence. He stepped onto the porch, his feet heavy, and knocked once, a tentative rap, then again, a little louder, urgency building in his chest. No answer. The house remained stubbornly silent.

His legs, finally giving way beneath the immense weight of everything he had carried, buckled, and he sank onto the cool, hard steps. The windows were shuttered tightly, revealing no flicker of light within. The silence was suffocating, vast and final, pressing in on him from all sides.

Had he crossed all those impossible miles, endured every aching step, every sleepless night haunted by longing, only to find the place empty? Was this it? Was his family truly gone... forever? Had he clung to a fragile, shimmering dream, only to watch it shatter into a million irreparable pieces in his trembling hands?

Grief swelled in his chest, a crushing, physical weight that threatened to suffocate him. The silence pressed in, vast and absolute, echoing the emptiness he now felt.

Just as the despair threatened to drown him, to pull him under into an abyss of utter hopelessness.

A sharp, startled gasp sliced through the agonizing stillness, piercing the quiet dawn.

His head snapped up, his heart freezing in his chest, then leaping with a desperate, wild hope.

At the edge of the walkway, frozen in place, stood Duy's mother. A woven basket of laundry, forgotten, hung limp in her arms, sliding unnoticed to the ground. Her eyes, wide with disbelief, locked onto his face, scrutinizing every weathered feature, searching for recognition. Then, with a choked cry, she dropped the basket entirely and rushed forward, her hurried footsteps a blur.

"My God," she whispered, her voice trembling, falling to her knees beside him, her hands reaching out tentatively, as if to confirm he was solid. "You are back. You're alive."

He could barely nod, his throat tightening with a complex knot of grief, longing, and an almost unbearable relief. He searched her face desperately for something familiar, something to prove this moment, this impossible reunion, was truly real.

"They're safe," she said, her voice breaking, tears now streaming freely down her face. "They made it to America. They're free. I have their address."

Tears, hot and silent, streamed uncontrollably down his gaunt face, tears of anguish for the empty house, but also tears of overwhelming, liberating relief. The house was indeed empty, but his family wasn't lost. They were somewhere, alive.

He couldn't speak, couldn't form the words. He just looked at her, broken and desperate, yet clinging to the lifeline her words offered.

"They're gone," she said gently, her voice full of compassion, sensing his unspoken question. "May... she waited as long as she could. She held the family together through everything. But after the war, the hunger, the constant danger... they left. She took the children and escaped by boat, like so many others."

"She didn't know what happened to you," Duy's mom continued, her voice soft. "No one knew. We thought... we all thought you were gone."

His legs shook beneath him, threatening to collapse again. "Did they... make it?" he rasped, his voice thick with desperation, the most crucial question hanging in the air.

She nodded, a wave of certainty in her eyes. "Yes. Duy told me they were taken to America. To a new land."

He fell to his knees again, but this time not from sorrow, this time, from a faint, shimmering glimmer of hope that pierced through the decade of darkness. His heart, though torn and weary, bruised by years of solitude, beat stronger with each breath. Each fragile beat was a confirmation that his family was alive.

A Message Across the Ocean

That night, in a small, cramped room behind her own house, generously offered by Duy's mom, he sat at a rough wooden table. Under the dim, flickering glow of an oil lamp she had borrowed, he picked up a pen with trembling hands. He hadn't written in years, and he had almost forgotten the feel of paper beneath his fingers. But his heart knew exactly what to say, what desperate message he needed to send across the vast ocean to the family he had miraculously found again.

He wrote:

My dearest May,

If this letter, against all odds, reaches you, it means I've been given a chance I never thought I'd have again. It means I am alive.

They took me so suddenly, May, in the chaos after the war. There was no time to hold you, to say a single word of goodbye, no chance to explain. Ten long, desolate years have passed since that day. I was gone from your side, but in my heart, I was always, always with you. Your face, your voice, your gentle hands, the way you laughed, the strength in your eyes, these memories became my sustenance, the lifeline that carried me through every dark moment of captivity. I survived by holding on to you.

I returned to where our home used to be, to the shell of the life we built. It's quiet now, terribly quiet, only the bare walls remain, scarred by time and absence. But standing there, amidst the overgrown garden and the silent rooms, I could still feel your presence, strong and clear, like a phantom warmth.

Then, a miracle. I saw Mrs. Tran, our neighbor. She told me everything, how you survived the chaos, how you protected our children, how you waited and hoped for my return even when all hope seemed lost.

My love, I wept when I heard her words. I wept for the years we lost, for the burdens you bore, for the sheer unimaginable strength you showed. You were stronger than I could ever have imagined. You carried the immense weight of our family when I was unjustly taken from you. You raised our precious children, nurtured them, and guided them, enduring everything alone, in a world shattered by war. I am so profoundly proud of you, May. So humbled by your courage.

There hasn't been a single day in all these years that I didn't think of you. I whispered your name in the dark, in the suffocating silence of the camp, even when no one was listening, to hear it. I dreamed of our children's faces, faces I've never seen grow, but somehow still feel I know intimately. I wondered if they'd remember the sound of my voice, or if you told them stories to keep me alive in their hearts, a flickering flame against the encroaching darkness.

I'm not asking for my place back, May. It was never truly gone. I have always been your husband, always their father, in spirit and in truth. I only want to return to where I belong, beside you. I want to finally see our children's faces, to trace the lines of their growth. I want to witness who they've become, shaped by your extraordinary strength and unwavering love.

I am not the same man who left, my love. The years have marked me. I carry scars, both visible and invisible. I've grown quieter, perhaps, more watchful. But my love for you, May, that has never changed. It was my only light, my guiding star through the darkest night. It brought me home.

I'm here, my love. I am yours. I always have been. Forever, Your husband.

There was no return address. Just a letter, sealed with trembling hands and sent across an ocean, carrying everything he had left: his profound love, his desperate hope, and the unbreakable will to be reunited.

At the time, mailing letters directly outside of Vietnam was strictly forbidden by the government, a perilous act that could lead to severe repercussions. He couldn't send the letter through regular channels; he had to find a covert, dangerous way to get it out of the country. To do this, he reached out to Mrs. Tran, a woman of remarkable courage and discreet connections within the fractured community. She had relatives living abroad as refugees, and through this clandestine network, she became the crucial link that helped him smuggle the letter out of Vietnam. Given the immense risks, stringent censorship, and sheer logistical obstacles, it was nothing short of a miracle that the letter eventually reached May, though it took many agonizing months to traverse the vast distance and overcome the political barriers. Each week that passed without a response was a test of his fragile, renewed hope.

A Letter Arrives

In America, a decade of relentless effort and quiet resilience had left its gentle but undeniable marks on May. The once smooth contours of her face had softened, now framed by the subtle etching of laugh lines around her eyes, a testament to the joy she had found amid profound hardship. Silver strands, like threads of starlight, now wove through the dark hair at her temples, gracefully marking the passage of time.

Despite these changes, her spirit remained as vibrant and unyielding as ever. Her inner resilience, an unshakeable core of strength forged through war and migration, pulsed with undiminished energy. Time had left its delicate imprints on her appearance, but her essence, her unwavering resolve and formidable strength, remained beautifully constant. She was a woman who had weathered storms and found her calm.

One crisp spring morning, amidst the usual flurry of household routines and the distant sounds of Anaheim awakening, a letter arrived. It was unlike any other. The envelope was yellowed with age, its edges soft and worn from a journey that seemed to span worlds. It bore unfamiliar Vietnamese stamps, their faded colors a stark contrast to the crisp American postal marks. Most strikingly, it had no return address.

May picked it up, her fingers tracing the faint scent of foreign paper. A tremor ran through her as she hesitated, the letter feeling impossibly heavy in her hand. It represented the staggering possibility of everything she had quietly waited for, a hope she had nurtured with stubborn certainty for so long, but never fully confronted. For years, she had carried the belief that he was still alive, somewhere in Vietnam, waiting, enduring, destined to return to her. She had never truly accepted his absence as final.

But the fear she felt wasn't whether he was alive. Her spirit had always known that. The fear lay in what this letter might truly mean. What if the words within shattered the fragile hope she had held onto for so long? What if they confirmed that he was alive, yet the reality of his return was far different from the idealized reunion she had played out in her dreams? Perhaps he had changed irreparably,

272

hardened by his experiences. Maybe he had a reason, a terrible, unspoken reason, for staying away so long. The fear of confronting a truth that could disrupt the carefully constructed world she had built for herself and her children was paralyzing.

Her hesitation wasn't rooted in doubt of his survival, but in the crushing fear that this letter could bring a truth she wasn't ready to handle. A truth that could fundamentally alter everything she had come to believe about her life, her future, and the resilient strength she had derived from the very hope she now held in her hands. Opening the letter meant facing a moment that would either validate her deepest hope or challenge it in ways she couldn't yet fathom, demanding an emotional reckoning she had never faced before.

And now, after all these years of silent waiting, after a decade that had stretched into eternity... the letter had found her.

May couldn't speak. She sat motionless at the kitchen table, the yellowed envelope clenched in her hand, staring blankly at the paper as if it held the secrets of the universe. Sang, coming into the kitchen for a glass of water, found her mother frozen and immediately sensed the shift in the air. Concern etched her young face. Sang knelt beside her mother, taking her hand.

"Mama? What is it? What's wrong?" she asked, her voice soft with worry.

May opened her mouth, her lips parting, but no sound came out. Her throat felt tight, dry. Her hands trembled uncontrollably as she passed the letter to Sang, holding it out with fragile, almost desperate hope, as if she were offering a delicate piece of her very soul. Slowly, cautiously, Sang took the worn envelope. She carefully unsealed it, unfolding the letter, her eyes scanning the faded ink. Her expression shifted from confusion to disbelief, then deep, blossoming awe.

Her lips trembled, barely able to form the words aloud, her voice a soft, awe-struck whisper.

"Mom... It's Ba. He's alive."

Suddenly, the floodgates broke open, the control May had maintained for a decade shattered instantly. Uncontrollable tears poured down her cheeks, a torrent of grief, relief, joy, and sorrow all mixing into one overwhelming deluge. Sang couldn't grasp every detail, every nuance of the letter, but one truth hit her like a tidal wave: their father, the man they had mourned as lost, was alive.

As the emotional aftermath settled for May and Sang, a new narrative began to unfold, one of displacement and new beginnings.

Chapter 24

"New Frontiers"

For May, the letter arrived like a quiet storm, stirring old memories and raising new questions; it meant hope. Or perhaps just more uncertainty.

Minh, meanwhile, had already taken a different path. He had been living in Texas for over a year now. There, his life began to retake shape. Amid endless roads, shimmering heat, and the steady rhythm of his work, he slowly found his footing in a place that offered both freedom and challenge.

The very name resonated with vast, open promise, a stark contrast to the tighter, more defined confines of his previous life. He drove into Houston, a city that unfolded before him in a sprawling tapestry of concrete and green, its humid air thick with the scent of possibility and the distant, ceaseless hum of countless lives intersecting. The endless highways stretched out like veins, carrying him deeper into this new, formidable landscape.

Settling into his new, slightly sparse apartment, Minh found himself in a neighborhood buzzing with a different kind of energy, louder, more expansive, yet still holding pockets of quiet. It wasn't long before he stumbled upon a local Vietnamese grocery store, a vibrant beacon of familiarity in the vast urban expanse. The moment he stepped inside, the potent, comforting aroma of fish sauce, fresh herbs, and strong Vietnamese coffee instantly transported him. A wave of nostalgia mingled with the present. As he navigated the aisles, his cart rattling softly, a quiet, melodic voice broke through his thoughts.

"Excuse me, do you know where the rau muống is?" Minh turned, a slight startle turning into pleasant surprise. Standing before him was a young woman, her dark, glossy hair pulled back in a simple, elegant ponytail, a thoughtful expression on her face as she scanned the produce section. Her eyes, framed by long, delicate lashes, held a depth and quiet intelligence that Minh recognized instantly.

"It's over here," he said, gesturing toward a leafy pile. "Near the cilantro, just behind the bok choy."

She smiled, a polite curve of her lips that lit up her features. "Thank you. I always get lost in here; it's so much bigger than my old grocery store."

"It's easy to do," Minh replied, warmth spreading through him, chasing away the solitude that had clung to him since his move. "Especially if you're new to the area, or even if you're not. They keep moving things around."

"Something like that," she chuckled softly, a pleasant, almost musical sound. "My name's Linh, by the way."

"Minh," he offered, extending a hand. Their fingers brushed briefly, a gentle contact, and a flicker of undeniable connection passed between them, subtle, yet profound.

As they continued shopping, a conversation blossomed naturally. They spoke of the bewildering array of Vietnamese snacks, the eternal quest to find truly authentic phở outside their parents' kitchens, and, inevitably, their families.

"My parents were boat people too," Linh explained, her voice softening as she picked up a bag of ripe lychees. "They escaped Vietnam, just like yours, but their perilous journey took them to the Philippines first. We lived in a refugee camp there for a while, a place of temporary solace and quiet desperation, before Lutheran Social Services helped us resettle in Minnesota. The Twin Cities, specifically. It was a huge change, going from the heat and crowded camps to... the biting snow and endless white landscapes." She let out a small, wistful laugh. "They always talk about how different it was, starting from scratch. They worked so incredibly hard, building everything with their bare hands and sheer will."

Minh nodded slowly, a profound sense of recognition washing over him. "Mine too. Every single thing we have now, every opportunity, it's all because of their immense sacrifices."

A comfortable silence fell between them, not awkward, but filled with unspoken understanding. The shared history, the struggles of their refugee parents, and the cultural expectations only someone with their background could truly grasp, all of it was there, silently binding them. For the first time since arriving in Houston, Minh felt a deep sense of belonging. It was a quiet echo of home, a familiar soul in a place so overwhelmingly new. Looking at Linh, he knew with surprising certainty that this chance encounter was more than just a polite conversation; it was the quiet, auspicious beginning of something truly significant.

Over the next few weeks, their initial, casual meetings turned into eagerly anticipated plans. Coffee shop visits became cherished rituals, where they talked for hours. The rich scent of roasted beans mingled with the growing connection between them. They shared stories of childhood in a new land, the intricate dance of cultural expectations, and the unique challenges of bridging two distinct worlds. Linh spoke vividly of the crisp Minnesota winters, the tight-knit Vietnamese community she grew up in, and her dreams for the future. Minh recounted his journey, his adjustment to life in Texas, and the aspirations that drove him. Each conversation peeled back another layer, revealing shared perspectives, mutual respect, and a comforting familiarity that felt surprisingly deep.

Then came dinner, a special occasion at a small, unassuming Vietnamese restaurant Minh had been meaning to try since he arrived. The subtle, aromatic spices of the phở, the gentle clinking of chopsticks against ceramic bowls, and the easy, genuine laughter between them created an intimate bubble, shielding them from the outside world. As Linh recounted a humorous anecdote about her very first, hilariously disastrous attempt at cooking traditional Vietnamese spring rolls, Minh found himself utterly captivated. It wasn't just her words, vivid and engaging, but the way her eyes sparkled with playful light when she laughed, the warmth that radiated from her presence, drawing him in. In that moment, amidst the comforting aroma of home-cooked food and the solace of shared heritage, an unmistakable realization settled over him.

It had only been a few times they'd met, a handful of hours in total, yet Minh knew, with undeniable certainty, that Linh was the one. Both were far from their families, building new lives in a new state. Both had lived lives shaped by strikingly similar beginnings, the extraordinary courage and sacrifice of their refugee parents. The echoes of their shared pasts resonated deeply in their present, creating a bond that felt deeper and faster than Minh had ever anticipated. Though it was far too early to be thinking of a shared life with her, a future together, the feeling was undeniable. It was her.

This conviction, however, came hand in hand with a flutter of nerves. That evening, Minh found himself restlessly pacing his small living room, the weight of his burgeoning feelings heavy, exhilarating. He needed to talk to someone who truly understood the intricacies of Vietnamese family expectations, the unspoken traditions, and the subtle nuances of Vietnamese culture. His mother, May. Calling her was always a delicate balance of comfort and gentle interrogation, but he knew she was the right person to confide in for something this significant. Yet, without a phone at home in 1980, reaching her felt like a monumental task. He would need to venture out, find a public payphone, or maybe ask a neighbor to use theirs. The public phone at the corner gas station was usually busy, and he preferred privacy for such an intimate conversation. He decided he'd try the next morning when the lines might be clearer and his thoughts more composed.

The very next day, after his shift at work, Minh walked with purpose to the familiar corner store where the payphone stood. He'd gathered ten dollars in change, quarters and dimes, that jingled reassuringly in his pocket. His palms were sweaty with anticipation as he dropped the first coin. The rotary phone's clicks and whirs felt unusually loud in the quiet afternoon air. The phone rang three times before his mother's warm, familiar voice answered.

"How are you, son?" she asked, her voice carrying over the distance.

"I'm good, Mom," Minh replied, trying to keep the tremor in his voice at bay. He began a general update about work, about settling into the new city, skirting around the real, significant reason for his call. As he spoke, he instinctively fed quarters into the phone, making sure the connection wouldn't drop.

A moment of silence stretched, heavy with May's unspoken anticipation. Then, a choked sob of relief, followed by a delighted gasp. "Really? Oh, thank God! This is wonderful news, Minh! And who is this person you met? What's her name?"

Minh chuckled, his nervousness easing slightly with May's immediate, unreserved enthusiasm. "Her name is Linh, Mom. She's also Vietnamese." He explained her background, the strikingly parallel stories of their parents' desperate escape, their journey through the Philippines, and the help from Lutheran Social Services in Minnesota. He spoke of their effortless conversations, the way her laughter brightened his every day, and the profound connection he felt with her , a bond he never expected to form so soon.

May listened intently, asking gentle, probing questions about Linh's family, her occupation, her character, assessing her suitability with the quiet wisdom of a matriarch. Minh answered honestly, his voice filled with admiration. By the end of the call, May's initial burst of excitement had softened into a thoughtful, approving tone. "You must get to know her well, but if you truly feel it's right, then it's good. I'm happy for you." Her words, cautious yet filled with a weighty blessing, brought a sense of peace to Minh's heart, peace he hadn't realized he was seeking.

The conversation with May, conducted under the watchful eye of the payphone, gave him a strange mix of relief and introspection. "Mom," Minh said, his voice softening. "Could you... Could you get Ngoc for me? I miss her."

A moment of shuffling sounds, followed by a muffled shout from his mother, "Ngoc! Phone! Your brother Minh is calling you!"

Then, a familiar, slightly breathless voice came through the line. "Minh! Finally! I thought you'd forgotten all about your favorite sister now that you're a big shot in Texas," Ngoc chirped, feigning indignation that quickly shifted into genuine warmth. "What's the news? Father's approval came through today! Did you finally get a real Texas cowboy hat?"

Minh laughed, a genuine, hearty sound that felt good to release. "No cowboy hat yet, but I do have something else to tell you."

A squeal of pure, unadulterated delight erupted on the other end, loud enough to make him pull the receiver slightly away from his ear. "Oh my Heaven, Minh! That's incredible! Absolutely, wildly amazing news! I knew it, I knew he'd get approved! Mama must be over the moon, jumping for joy! This calls for a celebration, a massive party!" She paused, taking a breath. "So, what else is new? Any Texas sweethearts? Or are you still just working yourself to the bone?" Her voice was brimming with playful curiosity, a teasing edge that made Minh's cheeks warm despite the distance.

He hesitated, a blush creeping up his neck even though she couldn't see it. "Well... there is someone."

"Aha!" Ngoc practically crowed, a triumphant sound. "I knew it! Spill! Who is she? What's her name? Is she nice? Is she pretty? Oh, Minh, tell me everything! How does it feel? How does it feel to fall in love?" Her voice brimmed with an almost dizzying mix of excitement and playful demand.

"Ngoc!" he protested, laughing again. "You should call me Anh Cả, don't forget our culture! Slow down! Her name is Linh, and yes, she's Vietnamese. She's... she's wonderful. And it feels... it feels different. Good different." He tried to articulate the profound connection, the feeling of shared history and understanding. Still, Ngoc's immediate leap to "falling in love" had thrown him off guard, making him stammer slightly. It was true; he was falling, slowly and steadily. But hearing it from her, so direct and unapologetic,

Ngoc, made it feel both wildly exhilarating and wonderfully, even hilariously, premature. He spent the next twenty minutes answering her barrage of rapid-fire questions, expertly dodging the more overtly romantic inquiries with vague smiles he knew she couldn't possibly see, but feeling lighter with every honest word he spoke about Linh. Ngoc, as always, brought a refreshing, unvarnished perspective and a much-needed dose of familial normalcy.

The news of his father's approval, intertwined with his blossoming feelings for Linh, filled Minh with a potent mix of relief and hope. The weight of uncertainty about his family's future had finally lifted, replaced by the joyful anticipation of reunion. And now, this unexpected, profound connection with Linh offered a new kind of future, one built on shared understanding and a deeply resonant history. As the click of the payphone signaled the end of his call, Minh knew that this moment, marked by the arrival of a long-awaited letter and the discovery of a kindred spirit, was not just the conclusion of a challenging year, but the exhilarating dawn of a genuinely new chapter.

The Long Road to Reunion

The initial shock of the letter quickly gave way to a surge of fierce determination in May. There was no time for lingering disbelief, only action. The very next morning, she immediately contacted the local Vietnamese community center, a lifeline for many families like hers. She also sought out a lawyer specializing in refugee family reunification cases, a name given to her through hushed, hopeful whispers within their close-knit community. The legal process, she was warned, would be agonizingly slow and incredibly complicated, but May's resolve was absolute. She would move mountains if she had to.

She became a whirlwind of focused energy, gathering every scrap of documentation that could prove their connection, their shared past. Out came the precious, faded marriage certificates, crinkled and soft with age. Old, treasured family photographs – the few they had managed to salvage – were carefully unearthed, showing faces now etched with time and hardship, but undeniably their own, as well as those of their children. Her refugee documents, bearing the marks of their harrowing escape, were meticulously organized. And, crucially, her children's birth records were compiled, tangible evidence of the family he had left behind and now sought to reclaim. Letters were painstakingly written, heartfelt narratives detailing their separation and the desperate hope for reunion. Affidavits were signed, sworn declarations cementing their truth. Countless forms, each demanding precise information and endless patience, were completed, filled out by hand with a steady, hopeful pen.

The U.S. resettlement program for refugee families had strict and often daunting guidelines, especially for individuals detained in the North. But because her husband had been held as a political prisoner in the "re-education camps," he qualified for a special immigration status under the Humanitarian Resettlement Program. This was a crucial piece of fortune, a narrow pathway through the bureaucratic labyrinth. With sponsorship from May herself, a testament to her enduring commitment, and robust support from the local church community and various resettlement agencies, the comprehensive application, a thick dossier of their fragmented lives, was finally submitted. It was a beacon of hope launched into the vast unknown. And then, the waiting began again.

It took another three long years. Three years that felt like an eternity, an agonizing stretch of days marked by an acute sense of suspense. Three years of May's heart leaping with every delivery truck that pulled onto their street, three years of checking the mail every single day, her hands trembling slightly as she sifted through bills and advertisements, searching for that envelope. Three years of fervent, whispered prayers, a constant conversation with God, asking for his safe return. Every single night, a poignant ritual she had maintained since the first day he disappeared, she would place a clean bowl and chopsticks on the dinner table for him, just in case. Just in case he somehow, miraculously, walked through the door. It was a silent, defiant act of faith, a refusal to believe he was truly gone.

And then, one ordinary, glorious spring morning, amidst the usual stack of junk mail and bills, a familiar, official-looking envelope arrived. Her hands shook as she opened it. Inside, a single sheet of paper, stark white against the yellowed memory of his last letter, bore the word she had prayed for, yearned for, and dreamt of for over a decade: Approved.

He would be coming to America. He would be coming home. The long, impossible journey was finally, truly, nearing its end.

Chapter 25

At the Airport

The day he finally arrived on American soil, the sky above was a muted, somber gray, as if even the heavens were holding their breath in anticipation. Early that morning, Minh and Hoang, ever the steadfast pillars of the family, had rented two spacious vans and carefully driven May and the children to the bustling airport. Just thirteen years earlier, their entire family had fit snugly into a single, well-worn Volkswagen Beetle. Now, a testament to the passage of time and the growth of their family, it required two vans to transport them all. Even in their hurried excitement, they nearly forgot the carefully prepared snacks.

May sat, her posture a blend of nervous anticipation and profound hope. In one hand, she clutched a crumpled letter of approval, its edges softened by countless readings, a tangible symbol of the bureaucratic hurdles finally overcome. In her other hand, she held a faded wedding photograph, its colors muted and edges worn smooth from years of being tucked tenderly inside her pillowcase, a silent witness to a love that had endured separation. Her heart, a relentless drum, pounded a steady rhythm against her ribs, marking the passage of time, each beat a silent prayer.

Would he still recognize her voice, softened by years and tempered by unspoken hardships? Would the touch of her hand, now etched with the lines of resilience, still feel familiar? Time, that relentless sculptor, had reshaped her. A scattering of gray now streaked her hair, and deeper lines had settled on her face, mapping the joys and sorrows of a life lived in his absence. But in this moment, none of that truly mattered. He was alive. He was finally, miraculously, coming home.

Ngoc's Anticipation

Ngoc, a whirlwind of nervous energy, sat perched on the hard, unforgiving plastic chair in the airport waiting area. Her legs, seemingly possessed by an independent spirit, bounced incessantly, a physical manifestation of the tempest brewing inside her. Her hands were clasped tightly in her lap, knuckles white, as the rhythmic hum of countless voices around her gradually faded into a dull background drone. Her thoughts, a chaotic flurry, swirled in every direction. At thirteen, she was old enough to grasp the profound weight of

291

the moment, yet still young enough to feel utterly overwhelmed by its enormity.

She had never truly known her father. He had vanished, a ghost claimed by the chaotic maw of war, just before she was born. All her life, he had existed only in fragmented pieces, the whispered stories her mother shared, often tinged with bittersweet melancholy, and the quiet, fervent prayers May led the children in every night before bed, always including his name. The man in the fading photograph, tall, undeniably strong, with eyes that seemed to hold a boundless well of kindness, remained an elusive mystery, a mere shadow she desperately tried to imbue with life through the infinite expanse of her young imagination. Now, today, he was no longer a shadow or a story; he was real.

Her stomach, a treacherous co-conspirator in her anxiety, performed dizzying flips. She found herself silently posing the same questions, a relentless litany in her mind: Will he recognize me? Will he like me? Am I what he hoped for? The idea of finally meeting her father, this mythical figure, filled her with effervescent joy, but it was inextricably intertwined with deep, gnawing fear. What if, after all these years of longing, he looked at her and saw only a stranger, a child he couldn't connect with?

Her palms were slick with nervous perspiration. She wiped them discreetly on her skirt, then darted her gaze to the large, unforgiving clock above the gate. The plane had landed. Any minute now, he could walk through those sliding glass doors, stepping out of her dreams and into her reality. Her breath came in short, shallow bursts, almost like she was trying to suppress an overwhelming urge to cry while stifling an uncontrollable bubbling of laughter.

Ngoc bit down hard on her bottom lip, a nervous habit. Her mind replayed the years spent wondering about him, the quiet ache of his absence. She remembered the nights she cried herself to sleep, tears silently wetting her pillow, when other children casually spoke of their dads. She recalled the countless hours trying to conjure the sound of his voice, the weight of his laughter, the comfort of his presence. Now, all those questions, all those unspoken longings, would finally be answered. But what if the answers, even after all this waiting, brought a different kind of pain?

Still, beneath the pervasive cloak of fear, exhilaration bloomed, spreading like a warm, invigorating fire. Her heart hammered against her chest, a rapid, hopeful beat, a drumroll for the imminent arrival. She was about to meet her father. The man she had dreamed about her entire life, the one her

293

mother, in her darkest moments, had believed was lost forever. But he had survived. Against all odds, he was coming home.

She sprang to her feet, a jolt of adrenaline coursing through her veins, as she heard the first murmur, then the crescendo, of voices belonging to the first wave of passengers emerging from the gate. Her breath hitched in her throat, catching, suspended. Any second now...

She was nervous, a tremor running through her. She was afraid, a prickle of trepidation on her skin. She was trembling, her entire body a testament to the magnitude of the moment. But above all, Ngoc was ready.

The Reunion

Phuong, Khanh, and Sang stood together in the bustling airport, a radiant trio of young women who had blossomed beautifully over the years, each a testament to resilience and grace. Today, they had dressed with almost ceremonial care, their attire reflecting the gravity and joy of the occasion. Phuong wore a delicate blue floral dress that fluttered with every nervous step, her dark hair elegantly tied back with a soft, coordinating ribbon. Khanh had chosen a vibrant, deep yellow blouse, neatly tucked into a crisp white skirt; her earrings caught the fluorescent lights, sparkling subtly with each hopeful turn of her head. Sang, always the most adventurous of the three, sported a bold floral print dress that mirrored the cheerful, almost disbelieving hope shining in her eyes. They looked poised and grown, embodying the young women they had become. Yet, in this profound moment, as they waited for their father's arrival, they felt a striking regression, like little girls again, their hearts pounding with the unrestrained excitement of Christmas morning, poised to tear open the most longed-for gift.

Every time a distorted announcement crackled over the airport's public address system or the distant roar of a plane reached the terminal, Phuong instinctively stepped forward, her wide, hopeful eyes scanning the incoming passengers. She approached one airport officer after another, her voice polite and soft, yet unmistakably trembling with barely contained anticipation. "Excuse me, sir," she would begin, her voice a fragile melody, "is that the flight from Manila?" She repeated the question with each new crackle overhead, barely understanding the rapid-fire words but clinging desperately to the fervent hope that, any second now, her father would emerge through the gate, stepping back into their lives as if the years had never passed.

A Father Returns

May stood nervously near the arrival gate, a silent sentinel, her children gathered beside her. They were taller now, so much older than the last time he saw them. Some already had tears glistening in their eyes, mirroring the emotion that swelled within her. The loudspeaker, a harbinger of destiny, crackled to life once more: "Flight 706 from Manila, now arriving."

May took the first step forward, slowly, almost tentatively, as if her body, scarred by years of longing and disbelief, couldn't quite trust the miracle unfolding before her eyes. Her lips trembled uncontrollably, and her voice, a silent scream of emotion, was caught somewhere deep inside her chest, lodged between relief and raw pain. She didn't cry. Not yet. She wouldn't allow herself to, not until she was absolutely, unequivocally sure.

And then, he appeared. The man stood still, his well-traveled suitcase forgotten at his side, his eyes, like hers, impossibly wet with unshed tears. He looked thinner than she remembered, older too. Time, that relentless sculptor, had left its indelible marks on both of them, etching stories of survival and endurance onto their faces. But the way he looked at her, with an intensity that spoke of years spent in darkness, gazing upon the long-lost sun, communicated everything words could not.

"Anh..." May whispered, the single word barely escaping her trembling lips, a breath of memory, a lifetime of love. And then, he moved.

He rushed toward her, his steps quick and urgent, as if he were trying to outrun the cruel years that had forcibly kept them apart. When they met halfway, in the sacred space between longing and reunion, a profound silence enveloped them. No words were needed, only the deep, unspoken bond of their shared past, a connection that transcended time and separation. He reached for her, his arms outstretched, and in that moment, May finally, completely, melted into his embrace. For years, she had carried the crushing weight of everything, a lone pillar of strength, holding herself together for her family, never allowing herself the luxury of breaking down. But now, enfolded in the warmth of his familiar embrace, she finally surrendered. All the immense strength she had meticulously held onto, all the unwavering resilience that had propelled her through the endless days, all the quiet, unsung sacrifices of the past, everything poured out of her in a cleansing flood.

She sobbed uncontrollably into his shoulder, her hands clutching the back of his coat like an anchor, as if she could hold onto him forever and never, ever let go again.

A Family Reborn

The children, a tableau of suspended emotions, stood momentarily frozen, witnessing the raw and powerful reunion of their parents. Minh was the first to stir, stepping forward hesitantly at first, then with increasing speed and certainty. His arms suddenly enveloped both his parents in a desperate, loving embrace. Hoang followed, his chin trembling visibly, tears now freely flowing down his cheeks. Long couldn't hold back his emotions any longer; he broke down in racking sobs as he rushed toward the group, joining the embrace. Even James, the youngest, stepped into the burgeoning family circle without hesitation, drawn by the undeniable magnetic force of his reunited family.

Chi, now a mother of three herself, gently pushed Charlotte and Isabella, her two daughters, forward, while tightly holding James, her son, closer to the man she once, long ago, called "Ba."

He looked at her with an expression of profound wonder, unable to speak, his throat constricted with emotion.

"Do you... know who I am?" she asked, her voice barely a whisper, shaking with a lifetime of unspoken questions.

His lips trembled as he reached a hand to her cheek, his touch gentle, reverent. "Of course, how could I forget?" he murmured, a tear tracing a path down his weathered face. "You're my daughter. My Chi."

Chi nodded, the tears finally spilling freely down her face, a release of years of unspoken grief and longing. "These are my kids," she managed, her voice thick with emotion, gesturing to her daughters. "Charlotte, Sang," she then lifted little Duy higher in her arms, her voice brimming with pride. "And this is my son. His name is Duy. He's your grandson."

He leaned forward, fresh tears streaming down his cheeks as he gently touched the baby's tiny, soft hand. Duy smiled, a pure, innocent, welcoming gesture, as if he instinctively understood the significance of this moment, as if he were welcoming his grandfather home.

Then, May gently pulled her husband into the very center of the group, and together they stood, one family, shaped by unimaginable distance and profound hardship, but now miraculously steady and whole. Around them, the airport continued its ceaseless, indifferent rhythm, a blur of strangers and disembodied announcements, but in their small, sacred circle, time itself seemed to pause, holding its breath. They held onto each other, not out of grief now, but out of quiet, profound relief, out of a love that had endured against impossible odds.

A Love Rekindled

As the initial surge of emotion began to settle, May looked up into her husband's eyes that had seen so much, endured so much, yet still held the familiar sparkle she remembered from their youth. It was as if the intervening years, the war, the separation, had been a long, painful dream from which they had finally awakened. A soft, knowing smile touched her lips, one that spoke of shared memories and a future now reclaimed. He returned it, his face alight with a tenderness that made her heart ache sweetly.

Later, in the quiet intimacy of their home, after the children had finally fallen asleep, May and her husband sat together, their hands clasped tightly. The silence was no longer heavy with absence but filled with the comfortable hum of presence. He gently stroked her hair, his touch a familiar balm. "I never stopped thinking of you, May," he murmured, his voice rough with emotion. "Every single day. You were my strength, my reason."

May leaned into him, resting her head on his shoulder, something she hadn't known for decades. "And you, Anh," she whispered back, her voice thick with renewed love. "You were always in my heart. Every prayer was for your return."

They spoke little of the hardships, the painful details of his captivity, or her struggles alone. Instead, they talked about the children, their growth, their quirks, and their dreams. They spoke of the simple joys they would now rediscover, shared meals, quiet evenings, the mundane beauty of everyday life, now infused with extraordinary meaning. In his eyes, May saw not just her husband, but the young man she had married, and in her touch, he felt the same resilient, loving woman who had promised him forever.

The years apart had undoubtedly left their marks, but they had not diminished the profound, unyielding love that had bound them from the very beginning. This wasn't just a reunion; it was a reawakening, a testament to a love that had defied time, war, and separation. It proved that true love, patiently waited for, truly does come home. Their happy ending wasn't a sudden burst of fireworks, but the gentle, steady warmth of a sunrise after a long night, promising endless days of shared peace and rediscovered joys.

About the Author

Sekip Surget is a writer with a deep interest in stories shaped by history, displacement, and the strength of the human spirit. With a background that spans both business and the arts, he approaches storytelling as a way to honor lived experiences and illuminate the silent struggles that shape generations.

Writing has long been his quiet pursuit, a means to preserve memory, explore identity, and give voice to those whose stories are often left untold. He believes that storytelling is not just a craft, but a responsibility.

To Believe in Freedom is his first novel.

He lives in the United States, where he continues to write, reflect, and seek out the stories that deserve to be remembered.

Acknowledgments

This book could not have come to life without the support, skill, and dedication of several remarkable individuals.

To my editor Alice – Thank you for your sharp eye, your honest feedback, and your steady guidance through each stage of this journey. Your thoughtful edits and unwavering support helped shape this manuscript into its best form. I am deeply grateful for your patience and professionalism.

To my designer, Josh – Your creativity and vision brought a visual identity to this story that words alone could never achieve. From the cover design to the layout details, your work gave this book a soul before the first page was even turned. Thank you for turning ideas into something beautiful and tangible.

To my beta readers, Sema and Murat – Your early insights, encouragement, and thoughtful suggestions meant the world to me. Thank you for reading with care, for challenging me to dig deeper, and for reminding me why this story matters. Your belief in this book gave me the strength to keep going.

To my wife, Nihal – I am deeply grateful for your unwavering support, thoughtful feedback, and steadfast encouragement through every stage of this process. Your belief in me and this story made all the difference.

Each of you has left an indelible mark on this project. Thank you for helping me bring this story to life.

With heartfelt appreciation,
Sekip Surget

Made in the USA
Columbia, SC
07 January 2026

77043118R00173